THE WOMAN CHRISTIAN CEO

BOOK COMPILATION

*Eighteen Entrepreneurial Journeys
Given by God Executed in Faith.*

Presented By:
Sheya Atterberry-Chisenga

THE WOMAN CHRISTIAN CEO

BOOK COMPILATION

*Eighteen Entrepreneurial Journeys
Given by God Executed in Faith.*

Table of Contents

Table of Contents

Introduction

Get Ready...

In this book, you will be inspired and empowered to pursue your God-Given Business, Career & Ministry unapologetically. My name is Sheya Atterberry-Chisenga I am the visionary of this book compilation. Included are 18 powerful & influential women leaders who decided to share their journey of courage, transformation, and empowerment. This book is to let you know you are not alone and that many women have been where you are. This book will give you the tools you need to begin the journey of living in your purpose. I pray you will be blessed beyond measures, and every word you read will be planted as a seed of faith and believe the promise of God.

Coach Sheya Chisenga

CHAPTER ONE

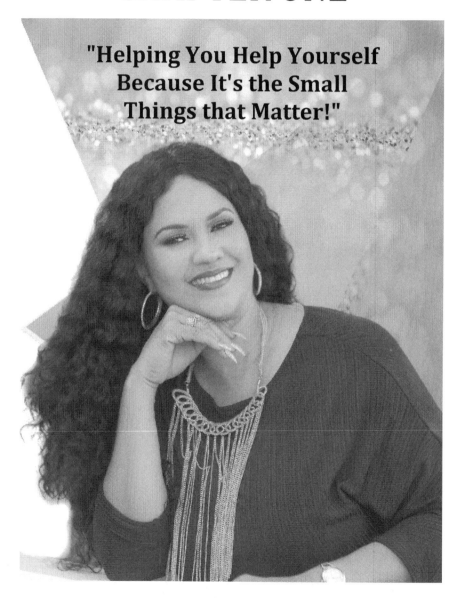

"Helping You Help Yourself Because It's the Small Things that Matter!"

Bridgett Marie Smalls, Author

There once was a time when I thought I had it all. I was married with kids, in the process of buying a home, had a job with the State of California, and three cars in the garage. Then one bad decision led to another, and my world turned upside down. I lost it all. I ended up making a decision at work that resulted in me losing my job, a $40,000 per year career with the State. With one click of a mouse and a little typing of some keys, I threw everything I had away. In a short period of time, I lost my job, car, husband, and home. I couldn't believe it. How could this happen to me?

I couldn't linger on the negatives of the situation. I had children to care for and could not let them down. I had to be strong. I knew I had to do better. So, instead of focusing on what I'd lost, I chose instead to push through it and make a better future for myself. I decided instead to use the entire situation as motivation to succeed in life again. My low point, my *breaking* point, became my new strength.

Slowly but surely, I was able to start rebuilding my life. It wasn't easy, and it took a lot of prayer, fasting and serving at church for me to get the hurt out of my heart in order for me to move forward. Eventually I was able to find another job, though the pay wasn't anywhere near as much as what I was making before. Still, the new job opened a few doors for me, and I was able to purchase another vehicle and find another place to live on my own. I continued attending the services held at my church and prayed to God to keep the hurt from my heart and to keep me moving on my path. I knew my prayers had been answered when I met a woman who would soon become a very close friend. We bonded as sisters in ministry and grew in the Lord together. There was even a calling in my life to minister to God's people, and I began studying to become a licensed Missionary with the Church of God in Christ. Before I could do that, though, the Lord had to do an inside job on me first so he could use me on the outside of me to help his people. So, I allowed God to restore my spiritual being. I didn't know it at the time, but He was also restoring me financially as well.

I began working for a call center while also working a part-time job on Saturdays where I helped my cousin teach classes for new business owners, something I had been doing since 2004. The call center position was very demanding and certainly tested my patience more than once, but it also pushed me to give my best customer service on every call. I ended up working at the call center for three years before unfortunately being released from my assignment. Despite the fact that I had gained full-time permanent employee status in 2013, the company I worked for began a partnership with a temporary employment agency which ultimately resulted in my termination. On December 3, 2013, I received a phone call from my employers stating that my assignment had ended. By this point in my life, I had reestablished myself financially, owned a vehicle again, and was even at a place of forgiveness in my heart only to lose it all again.

Despite feeling that my life was crumbling apart once more, I refused to fall into the same pit I found myself in the last time I lost everything I'd worked so hard for. I was no longer the weak woman I thought I was before. I was strong and independent, and I refused to go back to that place of defeat I'd found myself in last time. I was now a licensed Missionary with the Church of God in Christ, and I had sisters in Christ who loved me and prayed for me.

It is often said that the Lord works in mysterious ways. It just so happened that this was be one of those times. I received a call one day from the owner of the educational program I was teaching at, Golden State Educational Services, who ended up telling me that she wanted to sell her business and wanted me to consider taking it over from her. Though the opportunity sounded amazing, I was a little hesitant to take it. I'd lost so much already and had to work very hard to regain everything. Still, the opportunity was too good to simply pass up.

I thought about how hard things had been for me and the struggles I went through trying to maintain my peace of mind when I was looking for work before I owned my business. I felt a need to help others who were trying to help themselves out of the same types of situations. I knew it would be a team effort, one that would be made by myself and my future employees as well as with the help of my friends and the Lord. I believed that, with the help of God, the business would be a success. So, I set out to make a plan on how I wanted to run the business if I decided to buy it. I decided that I would Monday through Saturday from 9:30 A.M. to 6:00 P.M work each of those days like a regular employee. Whether I had class that day or not, I would come to work and work diligently from the star of the workday straight on to the end. Through my efforts, I hoped to be able to keep the business running and help it grow from where it was.

I also began thinking about what other types of services could be offered that weren't already in place. I knew we could offer the dealer classes, but I wanted to offer other things just in case DMV requirements changed. So, I decided that, not only will I offer pre-license dealer classes and continue to provide educational levels to dealers, I was also going to provide services to help others that may have been in the same position I was. I thought of adding resume writing, career building and planning, notary services, LiveScan services, corporation filing, and criminal records expungements to the list of offered classes.

After talking more with her and then with my sister in Christ, Diana, I called the owner back to tell her that I was in; I wanted to buy the company from her. She asked me if I was sure about it, and I told her that I was. While I wasn't 100% certain of how I would make this business a successful one, I believed in myself and my ability to succeed. I shared with her my vision for Golden State Educational Services, and she was very pleased with my plans and what I was going to be able to do with the company. And so, she agreed to sell the business to me.

I bought Golden State Educational Services in February 2015 and managed to build an incredibly successful business. I put my plan into action grew the business from being a $10,000 a year business to one that made over $100,000 a year. The purpose of the company is to open doors for men and women to become business owners. We offer continuing education classes online and in person. We also provide the education needed to become a vehicle dealer, and we also offer a full-service package where we can assist them in opening their dealership. We do it all, from A to Z. For example, my business offers a pre-license dealer class Monday through Saturday, and on Wednesdays, we travel to clients' locations. We also offer other services such as resume writing classes, wedding officiant certification, criminal record expungements, and more. We have a partnership with the California Department of Motor Vehicles, and I am an approved provider of vehicle dealer information for aspiring dealers wanting to begin their careers in the state of California.

My business helps form corporations, limited liability companies and more. We strive to provide our customers with a one-stop, all-inclusive experience. When people come to Golden State Educational Services, they can be assured that their dreams of becoming a CEO or owner of a small business is within reach. Golden State Educational Services strives to make a positive impact on our clients' lives. It is an honor to work with so many men and women from all walks of life and different backgrounds.

Being the CEO of Golden State Educational Services has opened many doors for me and my family. I am completely in control of the way I make money and how much of it I make. I control my own hours and days I work. I can now afford to take my family on vacations and not worry about the expense. I am in control of my destiny, and that feels good. Still, being the CEO of a business can also be quite stressful at times. I have so many people counting on me to help them achieve their dreams, so I must put in the many extra hours and days.

On top of the pressures I feel from others, there are the normal business-related pressures I must deal with as well. For instance, I cannot take a sick day at work and still get paid for that day. Luckily, after 4 years of business, I am able to reschedule things without losing business which allows me to take sick days, or even the occasional mental health day. Thankfully, God has given me good health, so I usually use that time off to help my family or to take care of my mental wellbeing without being at risk of losing my job.

The benefits of owning my own business have not only affected me. It's opened doors for my children. They can see the vision of the business and the growth it's had since I took it over, and they are already working in the business to help in taking it to the next level

In owning a business, one thing I have learned is that you have to give your all to it and believe in yourself, the services that you offer, and the products that you provide. If you believe in yourself, those around you will believe in you as well. You cannot second-guess yourself and your business. If you are going into business for yourself, treat the company like you would want to be treated, and don't forget to reward yourself for doing a great job. You never want to get bored and give up; you have to make up new ways to fall in love with your business and give it 100%. I love what I do. I am grateful to be able to help others get started with their businesses and see them prosper. I was able to provide educational services to over 250 students for the pre-license dealer class and to over 100 students for the continuous education class. I have been able to see these people learn the skills they need to become successful entrepreneurs in their future.

When I think back to when I first learned about the business being for sale, I'm often left in awe of how far I've come from that time. To be honest, my first thought as to who should take over ownership of the business was not of myself but of others in my church, or my friends and family who I believed had the money needed to buy the business. I envisioned one of them buying the company, and I would simply work for them within that company. My God am I so glad they said no!

I had people say, "Well, let me pray on it" or "Let me talk it over with my husband." Many people were hesitant because there was, admittedly, information about the business that I was not aware of at the time. I completely understood them not wanting to put $10,000 down on a business they hardly knew anything about. Really, the only things I knew about the company were the cost of taking it over, the services it already provided, and the needs of the people who attended the classes. At that time, I was unemployed, homeless, and unable to find a job for 11 months, so I am sure that everyone thought that it wasn't a good idea to simply hand over $10k to me or anyone I knew.

While I can attribute most of my success to my own self-confidence and sheer perseverance in the face of adversity, I am aware of the fact that the success is not mine alone. It was a team effort for sure, and that teamwork started before I even owned the business. When so many others were unsure of me and my ability to succeed at owning my own business, there was one that believed in me right from the start. That person was my best friend, my sister in ministry, Diana Martinez. She said to me, "I prayed on this, and I believe that you can do it. I can see you making this business work. Make the call." Diana, from the goodness of her heart and her belief in me, gave me a $5,000 loan to put towards the business. It was truly amazing that she was so willing to invest in me when I was at the lowest time in my life. Because of this kindness, I was able to work and make money from November until February 1, 2015, and I became the CEO and owner of Golden State Educational Services. And it changed my life.

Last year, I was able to go on three different vacations with my family. I was never able to do that when working for someone else. This year, we did two vacations and are planning on more next year.

I now have a legacy for my children and my grandchildren. I have stepped out of the box of my own comfort zone and am now living my very best life, a better life than I could have ever dreamed.

Golden State Educational Services is located in Sacramento, CA. We service the whole state of California and can help you to help yourself because we know that it is the small things that matter!

IT'S JUST ANOTHER GREAT DAY AT GOLDEN STATE!

Bridgett Marie Smalls, CEO
Golden State Educational Services LLC
6700 Freeport Blvd. Ste 105, Sacramento, Ca
BUSINESS PHONE: 916-395-7004
CELLULAR PHONE: 916-271-8990
EMAIL: goldenstatedealer@gmail.com
VISIT US AT WWW.GOLDENSTATEDEALER.COM

CHAPTER TWO

Don't Bury Your Talent!

Carolyn Tevis, Author

We are all born with a natural, God-given talent. I'll say that again, God-given.

I have turned my love of helping other people into a career, one that has been highlighted by the ownership of multiple businesses. Businesses that have allowed me to sustain myself, provide for my family and add to my community. I know from whence all of my blessings flow.

Put God first in all that you do, and he will see you through. Success, for me, has come from being centered in Christ. Being obedient and mindful of the lessons he continues to teach you is key. Always remember that the power of prayer changes things. Stay prayed up.

As a woman of color, you will be challenged, judged and critiqued, more so than others. Christian entrepreneurs are also held to a high standard of integrity. Embrace that. This should make you want to work harder to produce quality products and services.

It all begins with your ambition and passion to thrive. Tap into that passion and use your talents, your gifts, to thrive. In Matthew 25:14–30, The Parable of Talents, God stresses the importance of not burying one's gifts. We have a responsibility to use our talents for the greater good.

Being an entrepreneur doesn't happen overnight. It's something that you have to be driven and motivated to do. My journey to being a Christian entrepreneur started at a very young age. Both of my parents were entrepreneurs before I even knew the meaning of the word.

I grew up in a loving Christian home and growing up, my parents taught me the value of hard work. My father was a pastor and my mother worked in hospitality. My mother also kept busy maintaining our home and raising six children. My father made sure that we knew the importance of servanthood and serving the people of God. My parents instilled family values centered on faith, family, determination, and compassion towards others.

My mother was ambitious and wore many dutiful hats. She was our chef, nurse, cosmetologist, and family stylist. She started her first home-based business through a company called Lucky Heart, a cosmetic line owned by a Black woman. She also tried her hand with Beeline Fashion, which helped women achieve a level of independence by selling ready to wear pieces at clothing parties.

My sisters and I were delighted to be her clothing models, and my mother enjoyed the discounts. We were fashionable on a budget! Additionally, she started selling her fashions to our neighbors and to women at the church. She also explored a few other home-based businesses such as Presto Pride cookware collections.

My father was an Army veteran. Once he was discharged from the military he worked as a civil service instructor. My father also owned his own home-based business as a distributor for Mason

Shoes. I also remember my father and his brothers running a janitorial business. They would bid for different contracts and then split the work up between their families. We worked very hard to help clean and we got paid for our labor. My father was always serving and helping the homeless by giving them money and clothes. We would often give out food to the homeless at our church.

I had a colorful childhood filled with memories of family and church gatherings. I enjoyed primary and secondary school and I was eager to continue my educational journey after high school. I attended Sacramento City College. While there, I took some marketing classes which set the stage for developing my skills at selling a product.

Back then I didn't know that the word 'entrepreneur' would become a foundational pillar in my life. I worked fast food, but like my mother, I also explored some entrepreneurial interests as well. I sold Tupperware, Avon and Mary Kay. I was in-tune with the fact that I could work for myself. Chasing the desire to be my own boss, I sold fashion jewelry, organic household products and women's garments. I always applied all my efforts and energy towards my small businesses being successful. My determination never waned. I always believed I could do it.

My first job actually, was working in a convalescent hospital, that I noticed one day while walking home from junior high school. I was only in the ninth grade, but I went inside and applied as a candy striper. A candy striper is the term used to describe hospital volunteers, especially teenagers, who traditionally wore red-and-white striped uniforms. These volunteers had a long, storied history of dedicating their time to assist physicians and nursing staff. I enjoyed feeding and dressing patients and began to develop a knack for medical assisting.

After working at the convalescent hospital in that capacity for about three years, I decided to open my own licensed elderly care home. I was fueled to take on this venture because I saw how some of the patients were mistreated. I didn't like what was happening and I certainly wouldn't want my parents to ever have the same experience. I just knew I had to help.

The business was open for five years and offered me a wealth of experience-based knowledge. I had to learn the appropriate process for interviewing potential staff. I also had to learn how to fire employees with attendance issues. The elderly care home was a stepping stone towards my next business venture.

I saw a longtime friend at a grocery store one day and she told me about the opportunities in foster care. She shared information about a newly established foster family agency, and she asked me to attend an orientation to learn more about helping children. The class went well and I was motivated to become a foster parent. I worked with various children and families, reuniting some and others aged out of the system.

While serving as a foster parent for more than a decade, I studied and conducted extensive research to learn how to open my own foster family agency.

I worked double shifts as a Certified Nursing Assistant to save enough money to pay for the start-up fees. When it was time to open for business, my family was very supportive. My sisters, my parents, my children, nieces, nephews, aunties, uncles and special friends frequently volunteered to help. It was a blessing to have that kind of support. It kept my overhead costs low during a time when the agency was just starting and I had limited funding available.

I owned and operated the business for nearly 23 years. My foster family agency employed 25 staff members and placed hundreds of youth with responsible foster families.

I set up the agency as a non-profit organization, making it eligible for additional family and youth resources. I had comprehensive knowledge of custody processes because I had been a foster parent for 10 years. The state's guidelines are specific and stringent and having prior knowledge gave me an advantage in helping the children and families I served.

Managing a business certainly has its challenges. I never once used a business loan or grant to keep my business afloat. I relied on myself to make ends meet, by working hard and taking double shifts as often as possible.

Since the agency was a non-profit, it was governed by a board. Board members are critical to managing and running the business, because they can help you reach your maximum potential. In retrospect, after closing the business I realized that there were some things I could have done differently, such as hired outside help to oversee challenge areas. I learned that delegating is a good thing to maintain optimal work life balance.

God taught me a number of other lessons along the way, that I put into action. I suggest others follow them as well.

Lesson 1: Find Your Industry or Niche.

Every day God kept blessing me to find my niche. Love what you do and have the passion to thrive. Lamentations 3:22–23 says, "Because of the Lord's great love we are not consumed, for his compassions never fail. They are new every morning; great is your faithfulness." I knew I had a natural gift of helping others. I was less interested in selling a product, I wanted to assist people. My background selling products, however, was an effective foundation for developing my plan to sell my services.

Starting a business of any kind should be a spiritual journey if you are a Christian entrepreneur.

Deuteronomy 8:18 says, But remember the Lord your God, for it is he who gives you the ability to produce wealth, and so confirms his covenant, which he swore to your anchors, as it is today.

Additionally, Proverbs 16:3 says, "Commit to the Lord whatever you do: and he will establish your plan." Pray and ask God to show you a plan. It is vital to have a business plan in any business you choose.

Lesson 2: Research Your Market.

With any business, reaching your market is very important. You must be willing to put in hard work and your time. Volunteer in every aspect that you can. Learn as much as you can about the business. And that's what I did at first. As a foster parent, I learned as much as I could to increase my knowledge. Then I was an advocate for foster children.

I watched other people and how they ran their businesses. I had a friend who was in business for over 10 years before I started my agency. I worked under her for one year before venturing out on my own.

I'm an experienced advocate in providing services to children who have been abused and neglected. I enjoy the challenge of providing innovative solutions to care. I don't really want to put the word "market" on people, but it is what it is. Somebody has to do the work.

I'm so glad that God gave me the opportunity to be the CEO and run that business for more than 23 years. I served the organization in several positions and had a number of responsibilities including oversight of marketing. I oversaw and directed all aspects of the company from 1995 to 2010. I learned a great deal; which took me to my next avenue.

Lesson 3: Educate Yourself

Proverbs 4:7 says, "Wisdom is the principal thing; therefore, get wisdom: and with all thy getting get understanding."

Almost every day of my life I remember my dear father, Bill Hunt and his famous words, "follow instructions." His quote means a lot to me and is something that I pass on to others regularly.

In any business if you don't know something, you can always get help.

Educating yourself is very important, you're never too old to keep going to school and learning something new. That's what I did, and that's what I will continue to do. If you have breath in your body, God will bless you to do just that.

I went back to college after my daughter and my sisters kept encouraging me. In 2016 I received my associate degree. Educating yourself in any field and if you have a desire to progress and flourish, you're on the right track. The gift of help is very important in today's society. I worked in various residential care and foster agencies while earning my certificate from Alta Regional and the California Department of Social Services Division of Community Care Licensing.

Lesson 4: Build Your Business Slowly

"Lazy hands make for poverty, but diligent hands bring wealth," Proverbs 10:4

Anything worth having is hard work. Nothing comes easy.

Building your business slowly is another key component. This is another steppingstone to getting to the right level. I was in business for over two decades and was still constantly learning new things until the day I closed the doors for good. I served on the board of a private medical research and development group while consulting for several new and upcoming businesses.

Today, I run Roommates For Success, a business that helps the homeless find housing and resource services. I started slow and because of that I've had more than eight years of success. I've learned about the different resources that are available, the different components of doing this business. I learn something new every single day.

As a sister, mother, daughter, auntie, and now a grandmother, I feel that it is important to leave a legacy. We desperately need to leave something to our children and their children. It is a good thing if we can leave them an inheritance that will help them afford a home or other things financially. But more important, is to leave them with an inheritance in the things of the Lord. This is something that can never be lost. God promised that a godly man can touch thousands over the lives of his children and grandchildren. But to do so we need to be willing to invest, not just in stocks and bonds — but in a godly heritage that will take a lifetime to develop and prepare for our families.

Matthew 5:16 16 says, "In the same way, let your light shine before others, that they may see your good deeds and glorify your Father in heaven."

Making money should not be the only motivator for an entrepreneur.

Entrepreneurs must be risk-takers, whether it's in the form of financial investments, choosing employees in hopes that they'll help grow your clientele or expanding into an area where others have warned you against.

Entrepreneurs should be working to build something that will last. You should be taking the necessary steps to create a business that will, when managed properly, continue making you money well beyond the point of retirement.

Ultimately this journey is what you make it. Find your God-given gift. Don't bury it, let it see light, never stop learning and you will always continue to grow.

Contact Information:

Carolyn Tevis
Roommates for Success
(916) 862-8836
Email: teviscarolyn@gmail.com

CHAPTER THREE

**"Unstuck"
(Getting and Remaining)**

Gwendolyn Ware, Author

Recently I have gone through an "Awakening" of sorts. Many things have been made clear. The veil has been lifted; the blinders are off. My perspectives and ideologies have changed and the person that I thought I was no longer exists.

As a matter of fact, that person **never** existed, but was merely this unknown "masked" conjuring cowering behind the *real* me, the woman who was fearfully and wonderfully made, (Psalm119:14), and chosen specifically by God for a very *precise* purpose.

You see the enemy had convinced me of who I was as a result of my "circumstances". That I **was** my circumstances. That simply was not true. Nevertheless, I became so engulfed by so much fear that I couldn't even gather enough strength to peek out and participate in my own life. I believed the lies of the enemy and allowed myself to be consumed by the spirits of self-doubt, unworthiness, loneliness, and shame. The spirit of depression was so heavy and dark that I always felt as if I was in a deep hole sinking lower and lower while dirt was being heaped on top of me.

The lower I sank, the better I became at hiding behind this "masked stranger" that I had created to hide all the pain that was literally eating me alive. Behind the mask I was screaming and clawing to get out, wondering "why can't anyone hear me? I'm dying."

I eventually figured out that the problem was that I was waiting on *someone* to save me, instead of doing what I was taught, what I already knew to do, and that was to turn to Jesus Christ, who was born, bled, and died that I might be saved. How much more specific can one get?

As women, we often take on more than we ought simply because it's been ingrained in us that we are the caregivers of the world. We're responsible for everything and everyone; We are the backbone; We are the nucleus; We are the center, and the glue that holds everything together. Our families, our communities, our society as a whole depends on us to keep things moving in a positive direction. We are the nurturers. We bring and give life. We sustain life. But who will nurture and sustain us when we find ourselves overwhelmed and unable to keep all the balls we were juggling in the air? When they all begin to fall on top of us and feel like bricks or cement weighing us down? Who do *we* turn to when we begin to feel caged in with nowhere to go, and at every angle there's a 10-foot wall we have no possible way of climbing? We now find ourselves "Stuck", often times *trapped* by our own "self-imposed barriers" and inabilities. Inability to say "no", and/or to set boundaries, but most importantly, our inability to go to God for *direction*.

Now maybe this is not you, but in my own experience, the hardest lesson that I have fought and am still fighting to learn is giving up control, or rather learning I was never **in** control. I had to learn a very hard lesson about trying to control everything around me, every situation, every circumstance, every little aspect of my life. I discovered that I was not leaning on God and giving him my life. Not the way in which he requires. Although I had convinced myself otherwise. I believed that certain parts of my life I knew better than him. This of course was never true but humor me for a moment because it is truly amusing to believe that *you know better than God*. I had developed a very bad habit of giving things to God then turning around and taking them back. Though I didn't realize it at the time, this was something I did way too often. I was always there for everyone else, helping them in whatever way I could to get through whatever trials had befallen them. Be it counseling, taking them places, taking care of, and helping them physically, emotionally, spiritually, and at times even financially. I went over and way above at my job and worked way more hours than I would ever in a million years get paid for. So many times, all of these things were at my own expense and to my own detriment. I eventually became fed up and resentful, exhausted and severely depressed. My physical health began to suffer and eventually declined severely. But I kept a smile on my face and rarely let anyone know what I was going through, nor did I ever ask for help. I didn't want to appear weak, or as if I couldn't handle things since everyone counted on and looked to me to "fix" everything. (*The spirit of pride. We all know where that leads.*). (*Prov.16:18*). What's really funny is how I would counsel and give others advice on avoiding and/or getting out of the same types of situations I'd find myself in. (God has a very good sense of humor). I was *STUCK. TRAPPED* on the proverbial "hamster wheel", or "merry-go-round", as it were. I would pray God please help me; I don't know what to do. I don't want to do this anymore. However, whenever he would send me an answer, or provide a way out, I would ignore it and walk away in disobedience, because it wasn't the answer that I wanted, or it didn't look like what I expected.

Now bear in mind, that I had always been in church, sang in the choir, went to Bible study, Sunday school, belonged to several auxiliaries, and believed whole-heartedly in the death and resurrection of Jesus Christ. Yet I was still struggling and feeling like something wasn't quite right, something is missing. All because I was doing what *I thought,* all good Christians were supposed to do. Stay *active* in the church and *help* people. I failed to remember the part about *obedience being better than sacrifice, (1 Sam 15:22).* I was so busy with the *business of church,* that my *relationship* with God was suffering and I could no longer hear his still small voice because of all the noise and distractions behind everything that I *thought* I was supposed to be doing. (Prov.4:7).

I would later have to ask myself, "who are you doing all of this for?" Did God ask you to do all that you're doing? Did you even ask God? Lightbulb moment! You have never once consulted God on anything that you've been doing. You are being *Extremely Disrespectful.* You are trying to *play* God and do his work for him. You are blocking other people's blessings by not allowing them to walk their own individual journey and learn their own lessons. To fall and get back up, to *learn to depend* on God. To develop *their own relationship* with him. You're giving them *all* the answers and doing the work for them. God never once asked you to do this. I meant well but was way out of bounds. Someone very close to me once told me,

"Stay in your lane and you won't get run over." Well this is why I kept getting hit over and over again. My mind and body were battered, bruised, and worn.

I was finally beginning to figure out that my mom was right when she would suggest to me that "I was my own worst enemy". Not only had I aloud the lies of the enemy to overtake me, but I was also guilty of pride. I was *STUCK;* defined by the **Cambridge English Dictionary** as "Unable to move forward from a particular position or place, or unable to change a situation." I felt *TRAPPED, defined as "Groping, stumbling, unable to see our way forward." As a result,* I became isolated. The *MASK;* My conversations were guarded and rehearsed. I was very careful not to let on all that I was going through. I was so *BROKEN,* at this point I wasn't sure that I could be healed. All of these things *STUCK, TRAPPED, BROKEN,* and *MASQUERADING* as someone I was not, also lead to my making some *less than ideal* choices; adding to the list of *negatives,* causing further *SELF DOUBT, LOW SELF ESTEEM, INSECURITIES, FEAR, SHAME, ECT., ECT.* Every single one of these negatives were *Self-Imposed Barriers* that came about as a result of the *poor, distorted, static* filled connection that I had allowed to develop between myself and God. The static so loud with *Distractions,* that I could not hear the Saviors voice. No wonder I was drowning. After a while, *Depression,* had become my permanent address, the place in which I dwelled. I was so sick and tired of being *sick and tired.* Although I felt in my deep down in my spirit that God had more for me, (he had shown me glimpses through dreams and visions in the past), I had no idea at that point when or how it was possible for my story, *my life* to change. "O ye of little faith?" (Matt. 8:26). I thought that those dreams and visions were nothing more than my own mind creating what I desired my life to be. However, had my wireless connection to God not been obstructed by the foolishness that I chose to occupy my time with, (at times the tower was down completely), I would have recognized these as messages and encouragement the Lord was sending me that things would eventually change, and to not give up.

John 10:27 says: "*My sheep know/hear my voice and I know them, and they follow me.*"

How is your connection to God? Is it clear or distorted? Do you know/hear his voice? Do you listen/obey? Or do you treat it as if it's just more of the noise and distractions that you're accustomed to in your everyday life? I could have saved myself a great deal of grief by knowing the difference.

So "*HOW*" do we get "*UNSTUCK*"? Off the "*Hamster Wheel*"? Out of the "*Trap*"? What is the *Secret?* What is the *Formula?*

For me, the answers began to fall into place as a result of a *chance encounter. (*Nothing with God is by chance, i.e.; Esther 4:14*).* Through this encounter, however, I was reminded that time with God was not something that you "*fit into your schedule*", but rather he **is** the "*schedule that **everything** else in my life must fit around.*" In addition, I was reminded that my day should *begin* and *end* in time spent with Lord, praying, worshiping, and studying his word. This would ensure the lines of communication with God would remain open and free of static, providing clarity about God's plan for my life and the role that I would need to play in the manifestation of that plan. (Jer.29:11), (2nd Tim 2:15), (Jos 1:8). I would need to trust, have unwavering faith, and lose the spirit of fear. (2nd Tim 1:7). This would require me to *"show up"* and *"do the work"* necessary for me to *get* and *remain "Unstuck"*. This required a day in and day out, hour by hour, minute by minute type of commitment. Anything less would lead to *failure*, and a *return* to that *miserable*, yet *familiar* and *comfortable* place of *bondage* and *despair*. It would be a fight, a long road back to the land of the living, but I had to *get off life support* and *begin the process of breathing on my own* with the *support of the Trinity, (Father, Son, Holy Spirit)*, holding me up, I began to take *baby steps*. (Gal 5:1). Soon those steps became *leaps*, and I began to feel my whole *perspective change*. My *faith* was *increasing*, not only could I *see God's vision for my life*, but I began *to understand* it. It became *crystal clear* to me *why* I had experienced all that I'd gone through, and how it was all *linked together* in such a way that *God would* most certainly *get the Glory.*

These experiences led me to the conclusion that I wouldn't wish this on my worst enemy. This is a fight that must be fought *constantly* and on **Purpose**. Though I now know that we *All* must walk our own individual journeys in order to get what God has for us. However, there must be a way to *"assist"* others once they have reached that place where *they've finally decided that they are sick and tired*, want *off the "Hamster Wheel", and* that they are ready to *get and remain "Unstuck".*

With that, the birth of my *Life Coaching* business, *"UNSTUCK LIFSTYLE ENTERPRISES"* was born.

And so, my question to you is this; *"Are you, Have you ever been, Do you know someone" who is "Stuck",* and is fighting to become *"Unstuck"?* I now have a program available that will give you the necessary tools to *"Assist"* you and help you to begin those *baby steps* towards *moving forward,* as well as *equipping you to continue to move forward, embrace you journey,* and be able to *recognize warning signs.*

This is **NOT** an easy process. You must be willing to *"Show Up* and *Do the Work".*

Are you tired yet? Are you ready? Are you up for it? Will you accept the Challenge?

Pray on it. Listen for his answer. I'll see you soon!

Contact Information:
Gwendolyn Ware
UnStuck LifeStyle ENT
916-860-7337
Email: unstucklifestyleent@gmail.com

CHAPTER FOUR

Multiply Your Talents

Malia Kehaulani Taylor, Author

More than just an employee

Many years ago I got tired of working for different corporations, for very little pay. These companies were household names so I trusted them to be good to me, and provide for me and my family with secure long-term employment. But over the years I experienced lay-offs, office closures, decreases in benefits, and lack of promotional opportunities.

One year, upon returning to work from pregnancy leave, I was led into a room along with over 400 other employees. And we were all told we were being laid off because our company completed their newest merger, so we were no longer needed. No longer needed! I had just had a baby. What was I going to do? What was my family going to do?

I began to take a look at my position, my compensation, as well as my time there and asked myself, "How were you being treated by your employer? Did your compensation match your worth? Was your time considered valuable?"

And one last important question, "So, what's the difference between YOU and a big corporation?" Nothing! You're gifted, talented and have the ability to create wealth too! That was when I realized I needed to be more than 'just an employee'.

Early indicator of talents

Like many people, as a small child I was told by my parents to get a good education, find a good job and work hard. Because if you do these things, you will have success.

But no one ever mentioned that the God given talents I was gifted with already, could lead to even greater success.

Psalms 139:14 (New International Version)

I praise you because I am fearfully and wonderfully made;
your works are wonderful,

I know that full well.

At an early age I discovered many creative gifts and talents within me. My mother complained about the messes I would leave behind, from working on various art projects. And often said she could tell I was busy by the messy 'trails' I left. However, the finished project was always amazing.

And that creative urge has never stopped. Until this day, you can leave me in a room full of what appears to be junk, and out of those materials I will make a masterpiece. Yes, from early on, I was crafty, artistic and creative. I also began to discover that what I made with my hands brought joy to others. They not only liked what I made, they were even willing to pay for my finished product. As an adult I began to ask, "Lord, how does this translate into a career, business or money?"

When one door closes

A couple of years ago while still working a full-time traditional job, I experienced a new talent. Cooking Hawaiian food! Most of my co-workers loved Hawaiian food, but there were no restaurants nearby to get it. I grew up in Hawaii and the one thing I always loved was the Hawaiian food and culture, which I now had the ability to share with my co-workers. Being the oldest of five children in our family, it was mandatory to cook. I actually didn't think of myself as the best cook; I just cooked to get by. But everyone loved what I made!

Soon my employer noticed my talents and asked me to use them to help on fun and creative projects for work. I found myself making leis for upper management, and cooking lumpia and pork buns for my work team. And eventually I was getting orders for these items from co-workers on my days off, for pay! I was making extra money and making people happy at the same time, all while sharing my beloved Hawaiian culture and cuisine. It was magical!

But that year the economy hit rock bottom, and the employer I worked for closed their office doors and made us work from home. Although I still had a job, that extra income from co-workers was suddenly gone. I had discovered something I was passionate about and didn't want to just let it go. What was I to do now with this newly discovered talent?

Proverbs 18:16

A gift opens doors for the one who gives it

and brings him into the presence of great people.

A recipe for business

About a year after starting to work from home, I was still struggling with letting go of these new found talents. How do I move forward? How can I find people to share these gifts with? I was no longer in contact with people physically, as I had been when working in an office. Every day I would wake up, roll out of bed, log into my computer at home and start taking calls. I worked my 40 hours (or more) per week in customer service yet still had a longing to share Hawaiian food and culture with people. I felt miserable just sitting alone at home...like a caged animal. I wanted to be free. Free to soar like an eagle. And I wanted to be among and connect with actual people.

With social media on the rise, I started to use Facebook. I found it was a wonderful tool for keeping in-touch with previous co-workers, friends and family. Fortunately, over the years I've always maintained good relationships with past co-workers, friends and my community. I've never burned any bridges. This would serve my business in many wonderful ways in the future.

What if I reached out to all these people using Facebook, and shared about my cooking and creative projects? I had recently moved back to Stockton, California after being away for several year, and this seemed like a great way to test the waters, while catching up with everyone.

During this time God downloaded me with many visions. Every night, when I lay my head down to sleep, I was given information to move forward with my new business. My visions were intricate and detailed, right down to my company name, logo, and website design. I made sure I wrote down everything about the vision. Then I set my goals and came up with a plan.

Habakkuk 2:2

Then the LORD replied:

'Write down the revelation and make it plain on tablets

so that a herald may run with it.'

After months of toiling day and night, writing down these divine inspirations, while still working full-time from home, I finally had the courage to test my newest venture. I utilized social media to get feedback on what people thought of the services I would provide. I used pictures of Hawaiian food to entice them. Next, I gave away a free catered luncheon for up to twenty people, if someone could tell me why they loved their job. The winner happened to work for a local occupational health office. Catering the free luncheon at their workplace allowed me to speak to the company's administrators directly, while promoting my business as they sampled my product, delicious Hawaiian food at the luncheon. So much more effective than just leaving my business card at their front desk!

This was the start of my catering career. Even though I didn't know how to set-up the food for the luncheon. (I didn't even know how to light the little chafing candles under my buffet dishes.) All I knew was that I could cook and God had given me the stepping stones to being successful.

God equipped me with everything I needed to manifest greatness. By faith I would move forward day by day. I gained momentum and clients. I sharpened my skills and learned how to be the best in my industry. I represented my business and served my clients with a spirit of excellence.

In 2016, my business Hawaiian Legacy Catering & Design was voted Yelp's top 100 businesses in the United States and Canada. And I was able to visit the Yelp headquarters in San Francisco, meet their Chief Executive Officer and stay in a nearby five star hotel. What an incredible experience. I thank God for becoming the C.E.O. of my life!

Parable of the Talents

Have you ever heard of the Parable of the Talents (Gold) in the Bible, Matthew 25:14-30 New International Version (NIV). This scripture is a great lesson to us all in business.

The Parable of the Bags of Gold

Matthew 25:14-30

14 Again, it will be like a man going on a journey, who called his servants and entrusted his wealth to them. 15 To one he gave five bags of gold, to another two bags, and to another one bag,[a] each according to his ability. Then he went on his journey. 16 The man who had received five bags of gold went at once and put his money to work and gained five bags more. 17 So also, the one with two bags of gold gained two more. 18 But the man who had received one bag went off, dug a hole in the ground and hid his master's money.

19 After a long time the master of those servants returned and settled accounts with them. 20 The man who had received five bags of gold brought the other five. 'Master,' he said, 'you entrusted me with five bags of gold. See, I have gained five more.'

21 His master replied, 'Well done, good and faithful servant! You have been faithful with a few things; I will put you in charge of many things. Come and share your master's happiness!'

22 The man with two bags of gold also came. 'Master,' he said, 'you entrusted me with two bags of gold; see, I have gained two more.'

23 His master replied, 'Well done, good and faithful servant! You have been faithful with a few things; I will put you in charge of many things. Come and share your master's happiness!'

24 Then the man who had received one bag of gold came. 'Master,' he said, 'I knew that you are a hard man, harvesting where you have not sown and gathering where you have not scattered seed. 25 So I was afraid and went out and hid your gold in the ground. See, here is what belongs to you.'

26 His master replied, 'You wicked, lazy servant! So you knew that I harvest where I have not sown and gather where I have not scattered seed? 27 Well then, you should have put my money on deposit with the bankers, so that when I returned I would have received it back with interest.'

28 'So take the bag of gold from him and give it to the one who has ten bags. 29 For whoever has will be given more, and they will have an abundance. Whoever does not have, even what they have will be taken from them. 30 And throw that worthless servant outside, into the darkness, where there will be weeping and gnashing of teeth'.

Both the first servant and second servant multiplied their talents, but the last servant hid theirs in the ground. When the master came back from his trip he was elated with the first two servants because his investment with each had doubled. But the last servant was a disappointment because he didn't follow directions and didn't multiply what he had been given. He was even ordered to hand over the talent to the ones that multiplied theirs. You better use those talents, or lose them!

When I look back over my life, career paths, and job opportunities, I wonder what if I had recognized the talents in my hands earlier? Would things have been different? It took me years to realize that God has entrusted these talents from Him. They were given to be multiplied and ultimately glorify Him and the kingdom of God.

I started to see myself the way God sees me, multi-faceted like a diamond. He endowed me with many gifts and talents. And as I grew in my faith and walked with God I discovered, all of these talents were actually the foundation for my business and my future as an entrepreneur.

He has also given you talents to be used. Do not hide or bury them. Ask yourself these questions. What are the talents God has given you? What are the gifts that are in your hands? Can you identify them?

Proverbs 4:7

The beginning of wisdom is this: Get wisdom.
Though it cost all you have, get understanding.

Remember Y.O.L.O.

YOLO stands for You Only Live Once! If you want to live your God given purpose and feel fulfilled, ask God to multiply the talents in your hands. Ask the holy-spirit to give you insight on what those talents are and how to activate them. You will find peace, joy and love when you operate the way God created you. You are unique and there is only one of you on planet earth.

Matthew 5:14-16

14 You are the light of the world. A town built on a hill cannot be hidden.15 Neither do people light a lamp and put it under a bowl. Instead they put it on its stand, and it gives light to everyone in the house. 16 In the same way, let your light shine before others, that they may see your good deeds and glorify your Father in heaven.

God created you to shine! If I knew, back then what I know now, I would have started on my journey as an entrepreneur earlier. You're important to God. You're a part of His integral plan. You are His masterpiece! My prayer for you is to come into alignment with His plan for your life. I urge you to pray this prayer.

Lord, I ask that you multiply the talents that you have given me. Allow me to enjoy the process and live life to the fullest, reaching pinnacles and peaks that go beyond what I've ever hoped, dreamed and planned! Allow me to be used for your glory and not my own. Give me the strength to perform the day to day tasks you have for me. When I'm weak, become magnified in me. Give me your peace that surpasses all understanding when I feel pressure from all sides. Make me a good steward over everything you have placed in my hands. Help me to make firm and solid decisions. Help me to cultivate relationships that serve your purpose. Thank you for the increase and allowing me to be used in a mighty way. In Jesus name, Amen!

1 Corinthians 2:9

[9] *However, as it is written:*

What no eye has seen,
   what no ear has heard,
and what no human mind has conceived[a]—
   the things God has prepared for those who love him—

When you lay all of your talents at your heavenly father's feet, He will show you what to do with them. It is not by our will or our might, but by the power of God. As long as you're open, willing and able to receive what He has for you, God will open up the windows of heaven and slam back doors, that no man can shut. Now that you've empowered by God and by his holy spirit, go forth and multiply.

"I will give abundantly, receive abundantly and then repeat the process."

Contact Information:
Malia Kehaulani Taylor
Hawaiian Legacy Catering & Design
209.594.1648
Email: hawaiinlegacycatering@yahoo.com

CHAPTER FIVE

"The Blue Bike"

Celeste Bosley, Author

How did I begin my journey becoming an entrepreneur? The earliest memory I have of my entrepreneurship is when I was about eleven years old. I had my eyes set on my first bike— a beautiful, blue bicycle with twin wire baskets on each side of the rear tire—and I wanted to pay for it myself. My Daddy took me to Sears to at bikes, and that was the one I wanted; it cost $32.99. I planned carefully and decided to look for jobs I could do that would help me earn the money to purchase this bicycle. We had a neighborhood gardener whose name was Mr. Charlie. I asked Mr. Charlie if I could help him with some of the yards he maintained in the neighborhood. He agreed. Every Saturday, I would get up early and meet him at one of the yards he maintained. He was a meticulous gardener; each yard would be manicured perfectly. I learned how to be just as meticulous and make the yards look awesome, too—no weeds, bushes cut evenly, and I swept up the clipping and watered the lawns after we finished. I needed more money to reach my goal so I also washed a few cars to earn money. I even talked my Daddy into hiring me to make his lunch for work for $2.50 per week. I continued working very hard to earn enough money to purchase my bike--that beautiful, blue bicycle with the twin wire baskets on the back. I worked diligently to buy my bicycle. One day Daddy had to stop at Sears for one of his numerous home projects so I asked him if I could show him the bicycle I was saving to buy. We went to the sporting goods section and there was my bike—that beautiful, blue bicycle with the twin wire baskets on the back—and it was on *sale* for $26.99! I was a few dollars short, but after a long discussion with my Daddy, he agreed to loan me $6.50 so I could purchase my bicycle while it was on sale. I was elated!!! We took my bicycle home and with seven other siblings, you can only guess that they would all want to ride my beautiful new bike. So, I had another wonderful business idea! I posted a sign by the back door that read "Bike rides $.25 up and down the hill once." I felt pretty good about my decision to recoup some of the money I spent on my *own* bicycle. Unfortunately, the concept was short lived. Mama said, "No way, you will not charge your sisters and brothers to ride your bike." However, with that first fail was the beginning of my entrepreneurial journey!

As a teenager, I had become completely able to earn cash for things I wanted. I was the neighborhood babysitter of some of the neighbors. My parents would not let me babysit for just anyone; they had to be someone they knew and who shared a love for the church and God's word. I babysat for some pretty prestigious families—I babysat Rev. Jenkins of "Jenkin's Bar b que" grandchildren, the children of now Bishop

Ernestine Cleveland Reems, Maria Gardener Hamilton's children as well as other youngsters. I also worked at a neighbor's records shop selling all the latest Rhythm and Blues and Gospel music. I enjoyed making people happy by providing music to add to their personal collection. At the ripe old age of 15, I received my first printed check at a job; I was hired at McDonald's *and* Jack N the Box. I wanted more hours, so I extended myself and applied for work at Oakland's popular Kwik Way Hamburgers. I made sure that I kept money in my pocket!

In the coming years, I became a Tupperware Representative and Amway Distributor. I was a Melaluca Representative/Distributor and sold specialty gifts under the business name of Unique Gifts 4 You. These ventures were not the success I planned for them to be. I was selling products that by all accounts would be very useful and helpful to all consumers; some of them required sharing the business opportunity with others as this was the way to ensure residual income. Although I felt these were great opportunities for an individual to earn extra income and wonderful helpful products anyone could use, I always felt that my audience was not truly interested. I did have those that supported my endeavors. After a while I just ran out of steam because my all was not committed to the venture. It was not until I started providing a service that I was passionate about that I felt that commitment and relevance to what I was doing for others. The fact that there was compensation available for the service was icing on the cake.

By 1982, I was the proud mother of two wonderful boys. I found myself alone and wanted to be able to support my guys the way they deserved. My personal tax preparer was a wonderful man that lived in the neighborhood where I grew up. I referred quite a few friends and family to his tax service. But then, tragically, he passed away and his daughter took over the business. Unfortunately, after that, many of us could not reach the tax preparer after tax season that year. This is when I realized importance of being able to contact your tax preparer *after* tax time and when I made the decision to become a tax preparer and be AVAILABLE to clients year-round. I took courses to learn tax preparation at the local community college. I followed up with training from HR Block. These classes prepared me for tax preparation with the skill and knowledge to be registered with the California Tax Education Council. I became a Certified Tax Preparer, obtained Tax Identification Number (PTIN) from the IRS, received a $5,000. Tax preparer bond. I officially opened my business in 1982! My marketing strategy included posting flyers in public places—libraries, message boards, work boards, grocery store information boards as well as boards in local laundromats. Word of mouth was also instrumental in growing my business. I created business cards on my dot matrix printer. Computers were not popular at that time nor were they as developed like they are today. I conducted my business as professionally as I knew how. This entailed SERVICE! Since I was living in Berkeley at the time, I made appointments all over the bay area where I would travel to client homes retrieve their documents, interview them to assist in their tax preparation. I would take this information and my notes back home to my office to prepare the tax returns. Upon completion, I would go back to my client's homes to deliver their taxes. Their presentation folder included completed Federal and State Returns in envelopes ready to be signed and mailed by the taxpayer, a complete copy of returns for their personal records as well as all documentation utilized to prepare their return. I prided myself in knowing the best filing status for my clients. Through detailed interviews, I would discover additional write offs that reduce tax liability. I also gave my clients tax advice that would reduce tax liability in future years. It was very important to me to get the best for my clients. Because I have seen so many young adults place themselves in difficult tax situations, my new taxpayers received special attention. I reviewed exemptions and filing status on their W4 with them. If they were self-employed, I assisted them in proper bookkeeping to make certain they got all the deductions available and made suggestions for additional deductions.

Over the years, my tax business has evolved to include bookkeeping, electronic filing, fast funds (refund checks printed in my office), direct deposit of refunds, dedicated office space and representation before the IRS in some instances. I also added notarial services as a Notary Public. I want to be able to serve my clients in as many ways possible.

In late 1990s, I became a Loan Consultant under the mentorship of a good friend of mine, Christopher Barcenas. There were no certifications or schooling required to become a Loan Consultant. To be a part of this industry, I just had to acquire the knowledge to get the borrowers the mortgage needed to buy their first home and to refi their current homes. The Real Estate industry was really booming during that time. Unfortunately, in times like these, there were predatory lenders that took advantage of so many; loan consultants along with predatory lenders were adding hidden fees that went directly in their pockets with no concern for the homeowners that put their trust in them. As a Loan Consultant I was successful securing loans for my borrowers without charging unnecessary fees and as a tax preparer I reviewed closing papers from clients during tax season that revealed these hidden fees. I learned many facets of Real Estate while learning the loan business—the terminology, the ever changing many types of loans available, property condition requirements to qualify for different types of loans, income/credit requirements, the list goes on! In the mid-2000s, after the catastrophe of Real Estate took place, home values went down by 50 per cent and many loans were revealed as less than legally appropriate. Loan Consultants were no longer recognized when it came to compensation; we had to have a Real Estate license to be compensated for loans. During that juncture, I decided to get my Real Estate Licenses. The satisfaction I felt working with clients ensuring they understood all the terms of their loans was rewarding.

The first week as a Real Estate Agent, I put my first property in escrow! When it comes to buying a home, it can feel overwhelming. That's why I try to make it easier for home buyers. There are a lot of decisions to make besides how many bedrooms and the location. There will usually be compromises that must be considered and/or made during the home-buying process. I work closely with my clients to ensure they take all aspects of the homes they are considering for purchase. I go above and beyond for my buyers to get them in the home they can be proud and happy to own. Ultimately, the buyers have to make the final decisions and be content with the outcome, but I am there to assist them with guidance, experience, skill and knowledge of the real estate industry. I explain each step of the process as we move forward. In real estate, time is of the essence; there are contingency periods to ensure we stay timely throughout the transaction. I help everything progress as deliberately and expeditiously as possible when entering a Real Estate Purchase Contract.

It has not been an easy road to entrepreneurship. I have had to endure a lot of negativity from friends, family and strangers alike. There was even negative input from myself! Yes, I would put in the time and money to see success only to see mediocrity at best. I spent money on marketing campaigns that yielded little results. The No's, failures and mediocre successes were many; however, I have always determined to improve my services by cultivating my skill, knowledge and execution. There are long hours dedicated to growing my businesses which include attending classes, seminars, workshops, meetings and webinars. I have developed the skills and techniques needed to keep my businesses relevant. I work to keep processes in place to make certain my services are available to those that need it. I continue to meet with my lenders, escrow officers and marketing team to explore new ways to broaden my services for clients. My search to discover new skills, staying current on issues and enhance existing processes is constant and necessary to survive as an entrepreneur.

I find gratitude and joy in every transaction I closed. The teams I work with are awesome from the Lender, Escrow Officer, Inspectors and of course my client. I follow up with clients long after the closing on a regular basis. This has created new friends and relationships with my home buyers and sellers. I will continue to increase my knowledge, exposure and skills in real estate while I serve many new and old friends.

My journey as an entrepreneur has been all about SERVICE! I realize now that any future endeavors I conquer will include serving others. I pray that God will continue to have His way in my business development. I have multiple income streams while I help other people and that makes me happy, even happier than I was when I purchased my beautiful, blue bicycle with twin wire baskets on each side of the rear tire.

To God be the GLORY!

Contact Information:

Celeste Bosley

Realty One Group

Realtor for Buyers, Sellers, and Investors

(916) 868-9535

Email: celestebosley@gmail.com

www.celestebosley.com

CHAPTER SIX

How to Become a SaSSy CEO:
Be the Chief Experience *Officer* of *Your* Life

Sharon Boatwright, Author

Since childhood, I've always been different from other people. I was creative and energetic and spoke my mind. I was bold and full of spirit and got things done. Although often told to be quiet, I finally recognized that God had created me to be SaSSY!

SaSSY is how I've become a successful entrepreneur.

To me, SaSSy means to be true to myself as well as be kind to others. A SaSSY CEO needs to be a successful leader, by which I mean three things: being able to lead others by setting an excellent example, being a productive team member, and also being able to be a contributing follower.

SaSSY means to be a multi-tasker, and also keeping my word. Yes, SaSSY can be risky, but risk taking is necessary to succeed.

However, while successful, I didn't have <u>purpose</u> in my life. I was making plenty of money, but I didn't have balance and joy. In my unawareness, my life nearly collapsed around me – I was risking my family and my marriage.

As a result, I was forced to reconsider how I defined success and what was really important in life. I wanted to remain my SaSSY authentic self, but also change my circumstances. I needed to operate in exceptional leadership and become the SaSSY CEO of my own life

(I define that as "Chief **Experience** Officer"). To do

so, I needed to learn (and re-learn) what was truly important, what I call the **Five Essential Truths**.

Five Essential Truths

Essential Truth #1: Importance of God

Even though I've long been a "believer," I had mistakenly thought that I was in control of everything. During my crisis, I recognized that God is in charge, and I needed to strengthen my relationship with God. But how?

I started by modifying my daily prayers, slowing things down, and reconnecting with God. I asked God to gift me with patience, understanding, strength, insight. I slowly learned to forgive myself for my mistakes, and genuinely forgive others who had injured me. I saw that I needed to focus my actions on what I COULD do and leave God's work to God.

Soon, I added in daily journaling. I wrote down what was troubling me, what my daily goals were, and what I could do to convey love in all things. I started taking better care of my body – becoming more mindful about nutrition, health, and humor. I recognized I needed to change who I was spending time with, shifting to more genuine and spirit-filled friends.

And I found it necessary to create my own intimate praise party with God. I make time every day to listen to my favorite praise and worship singers, and my favorite inspirational and motivational speakers.

I am now in continuous communication with God.

SaSSY Reminder:

Proverbs 3:5-6 (NIV) Trust in the Lord with all your heart and lean not on your own understanding; in all your ways submit to Him, and He will make your paths straight.

Essential Truth #2: Integrity

As a realtor, I knew that I had to practice professional integrity, or I'd lose clients or even my license. I already knew that it's vital to do the "right" thing even without anyone else noticing.

Howsoever, I began to see that it is also essential to have integrity _within_ myself. As I became more honest about my fears, insecurities, and doubts, I exercised and strengthened my authentic self. By asking for God's help, I improved the match between my _inner_ integrity and _external_ actions.

SaSSY CEOs have good character and know that self-worth cannot be compromised. SaSSY CEOs demonstrate excellence, diligence, loyalty, and stay true to themselves.

SaSSY Reminder:

2 Corinthians 8:21 (NIV) For we are taking pains to do what is right, not only in the eyes of the Lord, but also in the eyes of man.

Essential Truth #3: Support Influencers

Back when I still thought I was in control of everything, I was comfortable giving what I believed was "support" to others (although I really may have been an impatient know-it-all). But I was not very good at receiving support.

Even worse, I gave my power away by listening to toxic criticism from people who were not, in truth, supportive of me, my vision, and my growth. No wonder I resisted feedback! I had to reconsider who my Support Influencers were and let go of outdated relationships that weren't healthy.

Luckily, I realized it only takes a few key people to see *my* Miracle! Now, I surround myself with non-judgmental people who offer honest and helpful feedback, and who inspire, guide, and love me.

I learned that a healthy, emotionally supportive relationship is a two-way street. I've learned to request permission before offering feedback, and I actively seek out different viewpoints. I learned to say "No" when asked to do something I don't really want to do.

I also learned about the "1% Rule" (consider the possibility that negative feedback or criticism might be 1% true and seek insight/growth, but also <u>not</u> give 100% weight to every negative comment!)

Who are <u>your</u> Support Influencers? Who do you allow/invite into your inner circle? And who do YOU support? Chose carefully – Support Influencers should be trustworthy, so you are safe and encouraged to express your dreams, feelings and concerns.

SaSSY Reminder:

Proverbs 18:24 (NIV) One who has unreliable friends soon comes to ruin, but there is a friend who sticks closer than a brother.

Essential Truth #4: Service to Others

You cannot be a SaSSY CEO without being of service to others, including your family, clients, colleagues, staff, and community. Service to others creates harmony in the world and replenishes hearts. I think a SaSSY CEO should be like a favorite auntie: encouraging, coaching, and demonstrating patience to all.

We know the Golden Rule: *Do unto others, as you would have them do unto you.* Do you act kindly and unselfishly every day? If you maintain a serving heart, you are serving God and yourself too.

Service to others also helps us gain perspective on our own challenges, by growing our compassion and showing us that our problems are generally smaller than other people's.

Especially in these very challenging times, it's vital that we all reach out and learn about "others" too, and it's always valuable to stretch your comfort zone. Reach out– we need to gain understanding of multiple cultures and different viewpoints and help grow and heal the greater community around us.

How do you serve others? How do you give back? Do you support your church with tithes and offerings? Do you donate your time and energy to service clubs or other volunteer organizations? Do you "invest" your time and money at different levels: something local, community-wide, global?

The Jewish word, *Mitzvah*, is used to describe an individual act of human kindness, without the need for reward. Commit to do something for others, if not daily, at least every week.

Here are some ideas to increase your contributions to the world: champion a cause, help feed the homeless, drive a cancer patient to a treatment session, sing to the elderly at a convalescent home, tutor a child with disabilities.

SaSSY Reminder:

1 Corinthians 3:9 (NIV) For we are coworkers in God's service, you are God's field, God's building.

Essential Truth #5: YOU - Taking Care of Yourself

To be your best SaSSY CEO, you have to take care of YOU. Your mind-body-soul is your temple, and should be cherished and cultivated. Pay attention and balance your many aspects: spiritual, interpersonal, emotional, professional, financial...

Remember to do regular self-care (exercise, healthy eating, sufficient sleep, etc.) to replenish yourself.

Regular self-care evens out moods, enhances energy levels, supports higher productivity, and increases self-esteem and self-knowledge.

You are also investing in self-care when you practice the *Law of Grace*. The *Law of Grace* is finding compassion and understanding, rather than judgment, which nourishes our soul.

For your mind: Every day, make yourself **do** something you wouldn't usually do, and **don't** do something you usually would do. This grows self-awareness and keeps us from doing things just by habit.

SaSSY Reminder:

Romans 12:2 (NIV) Do not conform to the pattern of this world, but be transformed by the renewing of your mind. Then you will be able to test and approve what God's will is – His good, pleasing and perfect will.

For your body: To look and feel your best, you need proper nutrition, exercise, and attention to your health. Be mindful about how you present yourself out in the world, too, since a SaSSY CEO knows we are always on an interview!

SaSSY Reminder: *1 Corinthians 12:12 (NIV) Just as a body, though one, has many parts, but all its many parts form one body, so it is with Christ.*

For your soul: Practice daily prayer and devotion. Without God as the basis, all else can be lost! Find and develop positive fellowship among family, friends, and colleagues. If someone or something doesn't make you feel good or safe, STOP!

SaSSY Reminder:

Mark 12:30 (NIV) Love the Lord your God with all your heart and with all your soul and with all your mind and with all your strength.

M I C Principles of Success

I worked hard to identify and practice the **Five Essential Truths**. It took me some time to retool myself. As I grew to love myself, I transformed into a more authentic person. I found my way back to balance, fulfillment, peace, and love. But always, God has been the cornerstone of my growth.

I realized I wanted to go even further – I wanted to expand my transformation and play it forward to others. Eventually, I developed the technique I call the **M I C Principles of Success**. I love that **M I C** also means "microphone" - so you can amplify your best self.

I also include what I call "SaSSY Moves" – those bold, brave (some might say crazy) actions we are sometimes too scared to take. I encourage you to give voice to those ideas – and try new things. You'll learn a lot, even if you don't implement or succeed with everyone.

I invite you to become your own **M I C!** If you try the four simple steps below, I promise **M I C** can help you too. Amplify your voice, your life, and your vision, and you will become a successful SASSY CEO!

1. Create a **daily journal** for your eyes only. Journaling is your letter to God. Include your prayers of needs, wants, and desires of your heart.

2. Use **M I C Principles of Success** below to systematically consider options for your daily activities.

M I C is designed to invite ways for you to care for yourself and also put these ideas into practice in the world.

3. **Partner** with your **Support Influencers** to create daily or weekly **accountability**. Check in and support each other – you'll accomplish more and grow in new ways.

4. Do this for **30 days** – and don't let yourself reread previous entries. At the end of the month, review the entire

journal to measure your progress, notice recurring patterns, and unaddressed issues.

Motivate and Mentor

- What will I do today to motivate myself to be my best, strongest, most authentic self?

- Who can I coach, advise, and encourage today?

My SaSSY Move: I fostered three children (in addition to my own two) while working full time and starting a business.

Innovate and Inspire

- What can I creatively evaluate (or re-evaluate) today to find new opportunities and solutions to serve my vision?

- How can I inspire others today?

My SaSSY Move: I left a Fortune 500 company to start my own entrepreneurial business.

Commit and Communicate

- What can I do today to keep my agreements?

- How can I listen carefully and improve how I communicate today?

My SaSSY Move: I volunteered and was immediately elected chair of a major fundraising effort, hardly knowing the organization. Through my commitment, leadership, and excellent communication, we raised $100,000.

What's my SaSSY Move today?

- Write down one bold action you could do today.

And remember: **His Will, His Way, My Faith!**

This is dedicated to:

This book is dedicated to My Lord and Savior Jesus Christ who makes all things possible. To my Sassy husband, Alex and my Sassy beautiful children, A J, Monniece, and Crystall who saw me as Lil SaSSy and Big SaSSy and loved me through the retooling of my transformation. To My SaSSy momma, Grannie Dot & SaSSy sister Rosalind, Thank you for shaping me into the SaSSy woman that you raised and loved. My SaSSy Jewish Auntie, Ms. Deb, Thank you for believing in me and pushing me to be my authentic SaSSy self and the best editor ever. Sassy Coach Sheya, Thank you for the opportunity and I am so grateful for your direction and wisdom. To all of the SaSSy Women who believe in me and allowed me to be **Bold** and be my authentic self, I thank God for each of you. I love you all, Shaboaty

Sharon Boatwright Bio:

Sharon Boatwright is a high-sales realtor and founder/ owner of two entrepreneurial businesses: **Thee' Experience Catering** *and* **It's Always Personal** *event productions. Sharon utilizes the* **M I C Principles of Success** *to mark progress in her life. She is happily married and devotes love and motivation to other women yearning to achieve their divine destiny.*

Contact Information:

Sharon Boatwright

The SaSSy CEO (Chief Experience Officer)- Be your own M I C

(916) 825-4315

Email: iamthesassyceo@gmail.com

Social Media/Instagram @TheSaSSyCEO

CHAPTER SEVEN

**MY JOURNEY
(Process, Processed, and Processing)
Starting and Building a Business**

Vicki Mack-Williams, Author

DEDICATION

This is dedicated to first and foremost God who is my everything and my family who mean everything to me. This book is dedicated to all the people listed and others, whom I leaned on and learned from –it was from them that I derived strength to be me.

My Father, J. D. Mack (Deceased);

My Mother Nettie Mack;

My Children: Christina Williams-James, Isaiah Williams, Sarah Williams and my grandson Micah Williams-Clayton;

My Coaches: Sheya Chisenga, Aneitra Scott, and Rachel Edwards who saw something in me that I could not see and encouraged, challenged and pushed me into what God wanted of me.

The women and the community at the It's My Time to Rise Business Institute; and the women of God that I am called to serve in ministry.

My Tribe/Community

My tribe/community is a woman like me over a certain age with dreams, goals, and desires waiting to be birthed out. Just waiting for someone to come along to assist and encourage her in the process of manifestation.

****

MY JOURNEY

(Process, Processed, and Processing)

Starting and Building a Business

Today I stand in a place of process, I am being processed and working on the processing part. Today I have learned to turn my cant's into cans and my dreams, goals, and desires before me. Keep me in your prayers as I pray for you. So, let me begin to tell you about the process I have gone through.

I have always known since I was a child that I was meant to do more, to serve more, to love people more and to come along side as a helper. Somehow along the way between finishing school, getting married, raising children, church work and hurts, disappointments and tragedies that desire got turned to a very low simmer on the back burner. My dreams, goals, and desires were pushed aside by more pressing issues. Therefore, I felt behind the curve and would not ever catch up. But God!

I am not even supposed to be in this Christian Woman CEO book compilation. Even though I do not have the years of experience or even produced what the other authors may have done. I do not even know half of what they know. However, I felt a push in my spirit that said just do it and I will make the finances and everything else line up. He does not tell you to do something and not provide for the finished product.

My journey has been long and arduous. I have felt like giving up but in this season I cannot. Truly God has brought me this far and I believe I am going to have to run on to see what the end is going to be.

Actually, got more serious in 2015, children graduated high school; and off to college, I thought now is my time. I typed a list and arranged in the priority listing I thought best for me. Well then, I got sick and had three very serious illness attacks and one was meant to take me out for real. Attacked in just about everything on every hand from 2015 through 2016. However, God said that I should live and not die. Yes, I lived and did not die; therefore, with renewed determination set out to start getting back to my dreams, goals, and desires. It was a slow process but I can tell you I am way closer today than I ever was before to the completion of my list and have actually added a few things to the list along the way. However, when Sheya Chisenga asked me to be in the first book compilation, I dared to hope that it was the beginning of fulfillment. I actually thought that was going to be my year. 2017 was a turning point but did not finish all that I wanted. January 2018 came and I moved forward some more but I did not even make a dent in the list. In the interim, I kept praying and asking God for direction. I became a part of the It's My Time Business Institute and was blessed even though I am the least of the ladies even today. Although, I was blessed to be a part and learning a lot, getting more information and tools to push me ahead-I felt lost. Even though sometime the information was over my head, various ladies within the Institute took pity and were patient with me. They took time to talk to me, encourage me and show me in a tangible way to put all the data I gained to great use. I will forever grateful to these ladies.

2018 came and went. I attended various workshops; conferences and training all were helpful and much needed. By the end of 2018 somethings began to click for me and information previously given I really began putting it together. I had been second guessing myself and not stepping out of the shadows because of fear. I felt so small and insignificant. All the while praying, studying the word and asking God the who what where and how questions. I did not hear Him clearly I think but I needed to make some decisions and start and keep moving. I had to talk to myself and tell Vicki she was not leaving this earth without impacting, influencing others, and leaving a legacy for my children. I had to get on a path that even though I was terrified – I had to tell myself to Just Do It (like Nike's slogan). I could not stand still, I still fall down, but I keep getting on to fight for my dreams, goals, and desires every day. I have had small, medium big, and big successes which are relative to me. Why, because the other thing that impeded my success was to compare myself others and then I would be frustrated that I was not further along. I had to learn not to compare, to move at my pace, savor the successes and learn from the mistakes. Fall, down, get up and ask for help along the way. Being a part of the Institute has been life changing.

I had to learn the need to have fearless determination to keep moving forward in spite of my circumstances or myself. Some things came easier and faster to me and other things took me longer to comprehend and slower to prevail in. But I kept moving forward and I am pleased with myself and getting more done now than then. God is so good to let me live to see me starting to make an impact the world, influence others, and leave a legacy for myself and my children. I am writing, three book compilations down and one to go, developing a virtual assistant business; I am a speaker, coach and event planner.   More importantly I have learned that I am unique in my own way, a leader, loyal, and a lifelong learner.

The steps I needed to learn in the process of starting a business:

- Pray always and ask God
- Talk and motivate yourself to keep going
- Be purposeful and able to share the vision with someone else
- Answer the question of why are you doing what you do
- Intentional about where you are going with the business
- Create Goals (services to provide, financial goals
- Break everything down in daily, weekly, and monthly tasks so that you can achieve ore
- Project Revenue
- If you need help always ask someone –somebody will help you
- Creating Business Name
- Creating Business Cards
- Pricing Services
- Develop social media presence (which ones to you)
- Creating flyers, products, and services.
- Develop a website

- Coach and Speaker Sheet

- Ask why something didn't work

- Celebrate your successes large or small

I have so much more to learn about having a business; however, I am using all that I have learned thus far. My Coaches and others are helping along the way. I have that by being a part of the Institute so many of my questions get answered and I move forward in all my endeavors.

The place of being processed is happening every day. I have learned a lot about myself in just this year along. Not just that I am saved, sanctified and filled with the precious gift of the holy ghost but that I am a helper – someone who comes along to assist others achieve more. I love to see people operating out of a place where they are fulfilled. However, first and foremost, I am a daughter of the most High God and get my instructions directly from the throne room so I go where He tells me to go, say what He tells me to say, and most definitely do what He says to do. A servant leader is what I am called to be.

I am processing everything the good, the bad, and the ugly. Learning and applying the knowledge that I have acquired thus far.

I have often pondered the words Christian leader and leadership and few ideas and concepts come to mind. A leader or leadership requires that:

- God must be first.
- First Things First
- Prepare Relentlessly
- Everyone's accountable, All of the Time
- Surround Yourself with Great People
- Reflect, Then Decide
- Under promise and then Over Deliver
- Develop and Communicate Strong Beliefs
- Be Your Own Person (Woman)
- Loyalty: IS a Vital Virtue
- Stand Up to Bullies
- Treat everyone fairly
- Study, Read, and Learn dependently (acquire knowledge collectively)
- Organize Around a Clear Purpose

Best Practices are the things that work in just about any business. I learned a lot as ladies shared their stories of how they got to be where they are now. The things I have learned along the way are invaluable and served me well by letting me use successful ideas and see them in operation. Just starting out getting business cards sounds simple but I had to think what type, square or rounded edges, and colors who would think there are a thousand color variations, glossy or nonglossy, standard, etc. Just settling on a name that I felt comfortable with for me took six months. Creating a price plan took a while too because I did not want to price gauge but wanted to have my work valued at a profitable rate. The list goes on and all of the components of putting a business together. You want to have every T crossed and every I dotted. I learned that sometime you have to just go with what you have and it's ok. If you find out it doesn't work, then rework it and try something else until you are settled in your spirit.

Here is what I know for sure you must have in your business as a Christian Women CEO:

- Put God First in Everything
- Pray daily
- Study the Word of God
- Application of the word, His will and Way in your life consistently
- Surrender your will to Him
- Trust God's Time and His Process
- Plan the Work

- Work the Plan
- Wait on the Results (if you planted good seed – your harvest must show up)
- Do not compare yourself with others and do not compete with others –YOU are uniquely you.
- Know that we are not in a competition –we are all sisters and there is enough that everyone can have a piece of the pie
- Learn to build one another. If you are not edifying then you are destroying.
- Information is power –keep learning and growing.
- Be willing to share what you know to help someone else.

A CEO is usually the acronym for the Chief Operating Officer of a business, organization or other entity. As such that makes us all CEO's but as a Christian Woman CEO we are saying to the world that we put God first in our lives and that we serve from a place of ethics and integrity. We are Committed to serving in Excellence and expanding on all the Opportunities that come our way. We are in the business of serving others to reach their highest potential and see the best of each other.   A Christian Woman knows that God is with her, she cannot every fail (fall down and get up) because God will always be there to help her through the process. Nothing more and nothing less.

I heard Sheya Chisenga, my coach, say this several times over the years (I am paraphrasing the scripture Ephesians 2:10) that we have been created to do good works which God hath prepared in advance for us to do. We are all created to go "great works"

She believed and so she did. Learn to work that crown that we as queens wear. I saw a little girl with an oversized crown and I remember thinking but she got it on and is wearing it like it is the right size.

I leave you with this heartfelt piece of advice:

Put God first, get you, family, marriage, and family fully submitted to Him. He will not only lead and guide you. He will open up windows and doors just for you. Pressed down shaken together and running over... the blessings of the Lord are YES and AMEN!

My admonishment to you is to Get up and Get Going. If you make one step, God will work it out on your behalf. I tell myself that every morning during my devotions.

For having more faith in me than I had for myself at times, for being brave when it was required for me when I fell into fear and for giving me a kick in the behind where and when appropriate, and tender without being trite, I want to give a special shout out to Sheya Chisenga and Aneitra Scott for all of their encouragement and support.

I pat myself on the back for giving God first place in this business/ministry process. I thank God for giving me creative and witty ideas; for the lack of sleep I have endured at times and for not allowing me to quit and I am not shrinking back anymore. God is giving me holy boldness, confidence, health, and strength to grow in this thing. I ask that you pray for me, help a sister out when it is needed. Continuously praying that all of the Christian Woman CEOs be blessed to prosper in their businesses. I am still the least of you all but I am growing and expanding as a follow in your footsteps. To God be the glory for my journey thus far. However, I am fully showing up each and every day. I am living life on full. God is showing me some "big" things and there is so much for me to get done yet. I am so grateful to each of you being in my life. Absolutely moving forward in Him.

This has been an amazing process going through the Christian Woman CEO compilation. I am learning more and more that I just have to do it and do it afraid. Stepping out in faith and moving forward. My motto lately has been keep it moving forward now. I want to be flexible and humble and seize the opportunities that God puts in my way.

I am so excited to be finishing my fourth book compilation. The devotional has been written and is currently being edited. In addition, I have written a book, currently, in draft form to be finalized. It has been a very busy and productive year! I give God all the praise. Baby steps for now and launching out more and more. Pray for me. I look back that I wanted to create other streams of income as I reach retirement and wanted to make a smooth transition after reason. Just look at God, He is truly ordering out my steps.

Currently, I have a Virtual Assistant business; I plan events, and I am available to speak at conferences, seminars, events and can provide training on various subjects. Also, I am a certified Christian life business and empowerment coach. In addition, I will be providing coaching to individuals, various groups both online and face-to-face. In the very near future, I will be launching out in ministry as well and will be soliciting your prayers, experience, and support. Let's have a conversation and see if I can be of assistance to you as well. In the meantime, remember that every good and perfect gift comes from above (James 1:17).

Some things to meditate on are a placard someone shared with me:

She Believed So She Did

You are humble

You are worthy

You are joyful

You are alive

You are confident

You are caring

You are loving

You are kind

Whatever you choose to be

You are happy

You are strong

You are able

You are loving

You are a work in progress

You are unique

You are brave

You creative

Life scriptures:

Jeremiah 29:11

II Chronicles 7:14

Favorite Quote:

"Our deepest fear is not that we are inadequate. Our deepest fear is that we are powerful beyond measure. It is our light, not our darkness that most frightens us. We ask ourselves, Who am I to be brilliant, gorgeous, talented, fabulous? Actually, who are you not *to be? You are a child of God. Your playing small does not serve the world. There is nothing enlightened about shrinking so that other people won't feel insecure around you. We are all meant to shine, as children do. We were born to make manifest the glory of God that is within us. It's not just in some of us; it's in everyone. And as we let our own light shine, we unconsciously give other people permission to do the same. As we are liberated from our own fear, our presence automatically liberates others."*

By Marianne Williamson

If you have any questions or require further information, please feel free to contact me.

Contact Information:

VICKI MACK-WILLIAMS, SisterKeeper

mereavickimackwilliams@gmail.com

vmackwilliams@yahoo.com

Website: Being designed as we speak

CHAPTER EIGHT

**It's All About the Journey!
Your Pain will not be in Vain,
if you give it over to God!**

Akia Holland, Author

"For I know the plans I have for you," declares the Lord, "plans to prosper you and not to harm you, plans to give you hope and a future."

-Jeremiah 29:11

In January of 2000 I was 18 years old and super happy to start my first year of community college. I was partying like a rock star not thinking of the consequences of my actions. At the beginning of my second semester, I found out I was pregnant by a man that I was occasionally sleeping with. We were what you call friends with benefits. When I told this "friend" I was pregnant, he had all the excuses in the book of why it wasn't his baby. I was devastated but could not see myself having an abortion or carrying this child for nine months to give it up for adoption. After dealing with the initial shock of me and my child being denied, I began to deal with the feelings of being disappointed with myself. Growing up I told myself I wasn't having kids and if I did, I wanted to be a in a happy, fun and supportive relationship with a person that loved me. I saw the stress, the pain and the struggles my mother endured as a single mother and I told myself I was going to do things differently.

My mother got pregnant with me when she was 17-years-old by a childhood friend when they decided to have sex one time before he left for the Armed Forces. This man, for reasons still unknown, never assumed his responsibility as my father. When my mother told my grandmother she was pregnant, my grandmother kicked her out of the house and told her "you made your bed, now lay in it." My mother found a maternity home in San Francisco. There she received the support she needed to finish high school and work part-time while pregnant with me.

19 years later, at five months pregnant I moved back to Oakland with my mother and siblings. We stayed with my grandmother to avoid becoming homeless. We started attending church at the same church my mother attended when she was 17 years old and pregnant with me. That's where I met a God-fearing, loving and preaching powerhouse, Reverend Regina Reese-Young. This woman of God took me under her wings and planted a lot of the seeds that are being harvested today. She gave me my first job as the church secretary and allowed me to bring my son to work with me. I brought him with me for two months before enrolling into the welfare-to-work program, where I received assistance to pay for daycare. Once I secured a daycare that I considered a good fit I started

looking for a vocational trade school in the medical field. I knew I needed some skills and fast, in order to get a job making enough money to get off of welfare. While attending the Medical Administrative Assistant program at Western Career College 4 nights a week, I worked two part-time jobs. The only way I was able to do all of this was because my Aunty Mako and her family helped me with my son. They helped me raise him for first 5 years of his life. They were the support I needed to obtain my certificate and start my career in the medical field.

In late 2003, I received a letter stating Nate the young man I got pregnant by, had petitioned the court for a paternity test. Once the results proved he was the father, I spoke with him to make sure he was going to be consistent in my son's life before I allowed him to be a part of our lives. My biological father was in and out of my life and I did not want my son to feel the same pain. I knew I could not make his father be there but wanted him to know I was serious about protecting my son. We decided we would co-parent. Over the next two years we decided to start a relationship, so we could give our son the two-parent household neither of us had growing up.

By 2009, we were pregnant with our second child and were living with his mother because of financial hardship. Around this time Nate's mother decided to move to Sacramento to help her daughter and grandson. She told us if we moved to Sacramento, she would help us as well, so we could go back to school and work. I was scared out of my mind to leave my family and my support system in Oakland and move to a new city. During one of many talks Nate and I had, he looked me in my eyes and said, "just have faith." This was odd because neither of us went to church and I had never heard him talked about God and faith before. But I felt something in my spirit and decided to take that step of faith.

Little did I know, moving to Sacramento was all part of God's master plan to turn my pain into purpose. I was without a job for 2 years. During those two years I volunteered at my children's schools daily. When I would show up to my son's school, the faces of his classmates would light up. I found this very interesting because I was one of those parents that would correct all of kids when needed. I never disrespected them, but I did correct them. Along with correcting them, I would play tether ball, wall ball and throw the football around with them. After a while all the kids in the class would ask me to come stay all day with them when they knew they were going to have a substitute; they didn't want the class to get out of hand or get in trouble. This spoke volumes to me because I knew they didn't like me correcting them, but it proved to me kids thrive off of structure. It also let me know kids listen once they realize you care about them.

While volunteering I discovered a lot of children in the class who were acting out just needed a little attention. After talking to some of them I learned some of them were in foster care and others were in homes with a single mother with little to no support. Their parents didn't have the support they needed to cope with the stressors in their lives, this in turn affected the children in a negative way. Statistically, families experiencing poverty, lack of resources, unresolved trauma, untreated mental illness, among other life stressors, are at higher risk for child abuse and neglect.

One Saturday morning I was sitting on my porch thinking about all the young black boys in foster care that aged out of the child welfare system every year, with little to no life skills, no resources, and no place to go. Tears started rolling down my face because I know how they felt in those situations. Then I got angry because I felt they were being set up to wind up in prison. I started talking to God, telling him how I felt and how someone needed to do something about this horrible cycle of events. That's when God gave me a vision to create an organization. I would house this organization where foster youth could attend life skills workshops, receive mentoring, receive counseling, and many other supports needed to create a healthier future. I started looking for work in the non-profit sector because I needed experience in that field in order to run my own non-profit organization.

On Craigslist I saw a position as an AmeriCorps Home Visitor. I reached out to my daughter's preschool teacher and asked her for help revamping my resume. I did not know how to formulate those transferable skills to show my experience working with diverse populations, my willingness to learn and my heart for people. Her helping hand lead me to apply for the position; otherwise I would have missed that opportunity to start my career over.

During my first year as a Home Visitor, I received trainings that helped me look deeper into myself, gain valuable parenting tools and become healthier emotionally, spiritually and mentally. As a Home Visitor I worked with a lot of young mothers compassionately- because I had been in their shoes. It was imperative that I did my healing work to meet these mothers where they were, not where my own hurt and trauma was. I worked as a Home Visitor for two and a half years; and along that journey I found myself a church home and rededicated my life to God.

This started the next level of revelations, healing, guidance and support for me and my family here in Sacramento. God revealed to me a clearer vision of working with young mothers in foster care and those who had aged out. He gave my idea for an organization a name and a blueprint. I typed my business plan up with so much excitement. I shared my vision and blue print with people that I thought would help me bring it to life. When I was met with little excitement and given no direction, I lost my excitement. I felt so hopeless I put my paper away and never spoke of it again.

I continued to work in the non-profit sector serving families with a heart to help them see a change in their situations. Three years later I received a call offering me a job to run parenting workshops for former foster youth parents, mostly mothers. I cried again.

I was asked to do something no one had ever done at this organization, hold a two-hour workshop. I was told I was chosen because they had observed me working with some of the mothers and liked how I engaged with them. I knew it was all God. I left that meeting in awe, thankful and mindful to always do things with integrity and love because I never know when God is going to send someone my way to help me along my journey. The scripture Galatians 6:9 became real to me in that moment. "Let us not become weary or become discouraged in doing good, for at the proper time we will reap, if we do not give in."

Two years into running the workshops, I was informed the organization was changing their policy. They were no longer going to pay independent contractors. This meant I was either going to provide this service for free or pull that business plan back out.

After a lot of praying, fasting, and marinating in God's presence; and a surrendered YES, my vision, It's All About the Journey Mentor Program, was birthed. Statistics say teen girls in foster care are 2.5 times more likely to get pregnant by the age of 19 and of those children, 50% of them will be placed into the foster care system themselves by the age of two. Research shows foster children that receive mentoring have had more successful outcomes. I am firmly convinced a mentor program that embodies Godly principles and is designed to help mothers could impact multiple generations at once.

I am grateful to God for never giving up on me and my vision. He has continued to position me in places to gain knowledge, build relationships with people that have gifts and the heart to help me bring my vision to life.

It's All About the Journey!
Your Pain will not be in Vain, if you give it over to God!

Contact Information:

Akia Holland

(510) 387-2761

Email: itsallaboutthejourney19@gmail.com

CHAPTER NINE

The Circle

Lashon Dorsey, Author

Humanity's identity must be wrapped up in our Lord and Savior, but His heart is wrapped up in people and family. It takes a village to revive, restore and release just one person, whether the person is the first one to attend college out of the family or you are the one who is taking the risk and going into business for yourself whatever it is, when the right people rally around you to make sure you succeed it changes the game. In the book of Acts chapter 14, verses 19-22 it shows how Paul and his team was teaching to a crowd that did not believe. Paul and his team were the minority and now he had been stoned and dragged out of the city hoping to be dead by the crowd. There are times in our life when we are willing to take the risk whether it is launching a new ministry, starting up a creative business or developing a new process. It takes courage, faith in God and a circle of people to aid you in your restoration and release!

As we all know a circle is a simple closed shape, it has no beginning and no ending; it appears to be whole and unified. The circle itself can consist of what you desire it to be, but for this section of conversation the Circle was very beneficial for me in business and building community ministry. Once you find your purpose allow God to cultivate it in your heart this component is very essential for your effectiveness and execution. It has been proven with many effective companies, ministries and organizations that systems, and strategies work to create a solid infrastructure for building. So in order to invest in people with a service or product that transforms their life, you must have a group of people that surrounds you with *prayer, business expertise, accountability, and collaboration.* As I was formulating a plan to launch Wellness & Fit I had a group of people who assistant me in learning how to do things just as simple as creating an email account. I had no idea how to do that, but the right people in place can show you and also teach you. Prayer will direct you to right people, at the right time!

Prayer is essential for direction and clear vision which allows you to stay focus on the purpose and calling. Prayer also gears you to have an understanding of your "why" from God. Once you are able to get an understanding your temporary wants will be overridden with your "why." This will cause you to have a healthy concept of services, products or programs you desire to offer. As you seek the Lord in prayer He will guide you to people as well as opportunities that are specifically for you. In order for Paul in Acts 14 to handle the magnitude of pressure in the mist of moving in his purpose he had to have had a prayer life, an active and intentional prayer connection with the Lord. Paul was very intentional creating onramps for people to learn and know about the Lord in a paganist culture he had to be bold, true to himself and keep the faith for the cause. What has the Lord told you to do? Is He giving you glimpses of your future or a new vision for your ministry or business? If you need clarity and boldness get into prayer, slip into a posture of prayer and stay steady in that posture until you have fulfillment. The people who gathered around Paul had to have known how to pray in that moment of death being expressed for Paul's outcome, but the circle gathered and Paul was revived. Prayer is the first important element of the circle which creates a solid foundation that will produce a ground for building.

Business is not a natural process, it is a whole different type of language. The business expert or experienced person deals with helping you learn the language, and infuses the process of systems that develops a plan of action designed to achieve a specific or overall goal, such as a blue print, game plan or approach. *The business expert* does not necessarily need degrees and certificates (that is a great thing to have), they may have a thriving business or ministry which they built from the ground up, which can offer real life tips and teachings that will assist in developing your process flow. A business expert is a professional who has acquired knowledge and skills through study and practice over the years, to the extent that his or her opinion may be helpful in fact finding, problem solving or understanding of a situation. A lot of us have the idea and feel the purpose in such an intense way, but the hold back in many cases is the "how to." How do I take my first step? What does the initial phase look like? How will people receive it? That was the case for me, for years I had an idea of assisting people on their wellness journey which includes mind, body and spirit. You cannot have a well body in a consistent manner without getting your mind healthy. I desired to help the African American population in which statistics show we die fast, hard, and young due to lack of knowledge, and lack of the "how to" to apply the knowledge to our everyday living. It is not so much in our DNA as it is in our daily choices that affects our live decisions. I had to connect with experts and experienced individuals who were on their journey, some had already past the phase I was launching out into. In this element of the circle you must be open to the challenge that will eventually get you to your goal. Even though I had the element of health down due to being a Registered Nurse, I needed help with formulating plans, processes, and strategies for the infrastructure of the vision. Setting up your financial components, from your banking system to how you allocate, and receive monies is a very integral brick to your initial building flow. As Paul took this endeavor in the book of Acts to speak and build into a culture that had no idea what the gospel was, and felt threaten to the point of hurting him, he remained steadfast and unmovable. Paul's focus was clear, his calling was made sure, and he was willing to be stretched, and challenged.

Developing the concept of your ministry or business through prayer is the first piece of the circle, then you have your connection with an experienced or an expert in the business field, next phase is accountability.

Accountability deals with how you answer to people who can assist you, i know this may sound different. How you answer to a deadline, or being on time to meet up with someone. It is your willingness to accept responsibility for your own actions. You must be committed beyond yourself and how you may feel in the moment. I needed people in my life in this area that was not afraid to hold me too what I needed and really wanted to do. When it got hard, and it indeed got hard, I wanted to quit or slow down. Accountability partners will put just enough pressure on you to keep moving. I gave them access to keep me on point, by being honest, letting them know my weaknesses and my strengths. Being truly accountable to a group of people or an individual makes you vulnerable and transparent, so again you will feel challenged and even uncomfortable. At this point in the game a coach may be very significant to have in order to get your mind functioning and driving at another level to house the flow and rhythm of your new business/ministry.

The circle can be very creative and specific for whatever your need is. Back to the book of Acts, Paul had his circle of people nearby. His inner circle dealt with building, pouring, and sharing the work of ministry as a unit.

Collaboration, being able to synergize with people, not just passing on a mantle; passing it from one person to the next, such as generations to generations, but working together with different viewpoints, concepts, ideas, and strategies to create a unique sharpening back and forth of the minds and hearts. In my process of collaboration, I had to be willing to assess and evaluate myself, my feelings, insecurities and motives. Why am I connecting with this person? What can they do for me? I learned from an individual who is yet still a part of my circle, to be so secure with ALL of you the good, the bad, and indifferent so that intimidation or comparison will not have a permanent place in the build. This allows you to connect and collaborate with people that are out of your league, have more knowledge, more money, and greater connections than you and you be okay with that. When you collaborate, it expands you with new ideas and connections, it also allows you to give space to other individuals to grow and learn as well. Collaboration can have different versions of itself, one of mines was hooking up with a business owner who specialty was cooking healthy food. One element Wellness and Fit offers when we do our 6 weeks challenge is an Eat and Learn evening event. The other business owner partners with us and demonstrates healthy cooking with information and provides us with a healthy meal to eat! The collaboration has broadened me and the other owner in a creative way that impacts the community around us.

As Paul laid on the ground after being stoned and dragged out of the city, I could only imagine how he was feeling, doing the thing he was called to, the thing he loved to do with a joyful heart at any cost. He was not received, he was mocked, and ridiculed for what he believed in; however, he was willing to put his live on the line for the cause of pouring out the gospel. When it gets hard, dark, and you feel like dying or giving up (the death of your goals and dreams) read Acts 14:20-*But the disciples formed a circle around him and he got up and went back into the city, and the next day he went on with Barnabas to Derbe.* (Amp. Version).

He did not settle when he was beaten, he took it, and his circle of intentional people covered him. He was restored to the point of going back to the place where defeat thought it met him.

I believe the right people in your circle can cover you, revive you, and restore you to press on into ministry, business or just to another level of life!

Contact Information:

Lashon Dorsey, RN, MSN-PH

Wellness and Fit

(916) 256-9625

Email: wellnessfit916@gmail.com

CHAPTER TEN

Distractions and Staying Motivated

Robin Robinson Myhand, Author

Becoming an entrepreneur has been a roller coaster ride for me. It's had its ups and downs, flips and corkscrews. I didn't have any role models in my family or circle of friends to help guide me, be a support, or a sounding board.

I started my life coaching business after I went on a journey of self-discovery and discovered that what I had been doing for a long time was actually something that could be a business. I took at class entitled "What were you born to do". When I looked at the instructor's bio, it stated "Life Coach". I began looking into what becoming a life coach would involve and moved forward from there. I researched programs and found one that fit into my schedule and my budget (just keeping it real). I loved it and did well on my assignments and final test. I received my certificate and then came the task of trying to start a business. Oh my, has it been an adventure.

Part of the class was creating a business plan. I had that in place but then what do I do.

The one thing that didn't take place in my training was creating a program and/or product. I learned how to guide a coaching session and help people dig deeper but that was it. I found a business coach, started taking workshops and creating programs.

I was given three ideas by GOD. It had to be GOD because they just came to me. All three came to me while I was taking a shower. This is usually where Ideas and messages come to me. I paid attention, wrote them down and then guess what? I got distracted.

I know I'm not the only one that has or will deal with this. So, what do I mean by distracted?

There are three distractions that I feel every entrepreneur will deal with on a regular basis. Even when you think you have moved passed them. You still get caught up. Here they are:

1. Shiny Object Syndrome
2. Comparison
3. Analysis Paralysis

I, like many entrepreneurs have many interests and ideas. Entrepreneurs tend to be motivated and are attracted to new developments and technology. We like to start new projects and create new things. I can think of all kinds of things to share and create where personal development is concerned.

This is where the Shiny Object syndrome (SOS) comes into play. SOS, is where you get side tracked by a new idea, project, technology, etc. and now you're off on a different trajectory from where you originally started. Just like when you were a child and chased after shiny objects. Once you got it, you lost interest and chased after the next shiny object. For myself and many entrepreneurs the SOS may be a website, marketing strategy, building your email list, technology, subject matter, product, how to get and retain clients, etc. and for some a new business venture.

Shiny Object Syndrome is the disease of distraction and the fear of missing out. You see something that you will need in your business or find information that you can incorporate in your business and that becomes your new focus or you think you should be doing something because everyone else (so it appears) is doing it.

I've been distracted by SOS many times thinking it was a shortcut to success. It looked like everyone was making thousands while I was making hundreds or hearing crickets. There was lint in my pockets. Money going out no money coming in. You get the picture.

I don't know everything and I don't know what I don't know. So here I go researching, creating a freebie, creating a course, how to write a book, how to grow your email list, marketing, etc. The emails start coming in because I've signed up on their email list to get information or have purchased a product. Facebook ads pop up that catch my attention promising to teach me everything I need to know. Sometimes the fear of missing out creeps in because I fear that I won't see the ad again and miss out on valuable information. Now my email is full, I've created multiple folders, I have too much information, I'm split between too many projects, I've taken too many classes, I'm overwhelmed and have totally lost focus.

Now that I have this information from so many sources, I start to compare myself to them.

"Comparison is the thief of joy"

Theodore Roosevelt

Comparison is one of the main ways to get caught up in SOS. I've discovered that I compared my real life and business to a highlight of someone else's life and business. Websites, Facebook, Instagram only show you the highlights. Websites are created to make you look professional and make your products or offers look fabulous. This means that the website designer and graphic artist did their job well. It does not mean that what is being offered is of quality and is usable. Most people post on the good things that are going on in their life and business. It's a snapshot. Many people don't have the perfect life we perceive them to have.

Comparing is natural so let's not beat ourselves up about it. It's how it is internalized and how we use it that makes a difference. It can be helpful, constructive, inspiring and motivating for you. If it sends you down in a spiral, then it's not healthy and you need to stop. One way to stop the spiral is not to see the other person as competition, be happy for their success. See it as proof that you can make it too. There is enough space in the world for everyone.

My comparison started with looking at other coach's websites to get inspiration. I found a few that I liked and made some notes. I looked at their products and programs as well and found programs that I was both interested in and might want to teach. I wrote out what I wanted to say on the website. I had a logo created, got a picture made, and found someone to create my website. That took a bit of time but I was focused and had it completed. The comparison was with what they offered and what I was thinking about or better yet what GOD had given me. I didn't see anything like what I had been given, so I started to doubt myself and felt that there wasn't a market for what I had to offer. Big mistake! I didn't realize until later that this is how I could stand out in the crowded world of life coaching.

I've compared myself into a state of Analysis Paralysis, which is the state of overanalyzing or overthinking information or a situation so that a decision or action is not taken. Decisions are prolonged in the hope of finding more information, a better solution, offer, or deal. Overthinking is a guard against failure or making a wrong choice.

The more data we have the harder it is to process it. Too much information and too many choices makes it hard to move forward with a decision. Too much = stress = no movement.

Overthinking kills creativity. It can bring on anxiety and less satisfaction with your decisions.

Here's the cycle of Analysis Paralysis:

- Idea – Analysis Paralysis (Overwhelmed due to too much information, comparison, fear, rejection) – I'll think about it some more. Repeat.

- Idea – Analysis Paralysis (Overwhelm due to too much information, comparison, fear, rejection) – I'll think about it some more. Repeat.

You get the idea. You are in a circle of overwhelm, comparison, fear, and inaction due to distractions.

So, what can we do about all of this?

Here is what I have discovered and a few ideas to combat these distractions:

➢ Entrepreneurship is a personal journey. We all have different journeys. It's not for the faint of heart and you can't compare yourself to anyone else.
➢ Get to know you as a person and as a business person. Self-knowledge is key. Work in your strengths and *develop a team* to help with the other areas of business that you need assistance with.
➢ Fear comes with Entrepreneurship.

There are several acronyms for fear. Here are a few. *The choice is yours!*

- Forget Everything And Run
- False Evidence Appearing Real
- Face Everything And Rise
- Face Everything And Recover

➢ There is no smooth road to success and there are no shortcuts. Don't live someone else's idea of success. Write your own definition of success. Run your business your way. Gather information (inspiration) from different places, but don't copy them. Do things your way so that you can establish your brand and voice.

➢ Write all of your ideas in one place (a journal or a word document), do a brain dump regularly and review periodically.

➢ Get clear on your business model/plan and stick to it. Stay in your lane.

➢ Determine where you are in your business. Do you need to work on a website, products, programs, book, speaking, building an email list, or marketing?

➢ Do things in your business that you enjoy. If you don't like to write a lot, then don't do blogposts or commit to a weekly email blast or newsletter. There are too many other options to get your message across.

➢ If you are a working-prenuer (a person working a fulltime job and also has a business), take the information you find and receive and tailor it to you and your availability (e.g., you may not post something in social media every day but can post 1 - 3 times per week).

➢ Shiny Objects will always be around. They don't help you to succeed and make you feel inadequate. They prey on your wallet and your time, shift your focus and make you doubt your own business.

➢ Set a timer for your activities. (e.g., checking your email, responding to email, social media, posting, researching, etc.)

    o Decide the length of time you want to spend on the activity

    o Set an intention – what do you want to achieve during the time

    o Focus – specifically on that activity

    o When the timer goes off, stop what you are doing

➢ Focus on one area at a time.

    o Limit the amount of information you consume and determine the number of resources you'll use by setting a time limit to do your research (e.g., 1 hour, 20 minutes on Monday, Wednesday, and Friday, etc. for 1 week, etc.)

    o Make a decision based on the information you have

    o Take a step to move forward and make a plan for completion.

➢ In order for you and your business to grow, you will have to invest in yourself. With there being so much out there in the marketplace this can get overwhelming.

    o The key is to stay focused.

    o What area of your business are your working on?

    o Ask yourself, "Does this help me achieve my goal at this time?"

- o If the information, book, e-book, course, workshop, or seminar does not coincide with what your focus is, then skip it.
- o If it does, then focus on the training and complete it before moving on to the next goal.

- ➤ Staying Focused is the key takeaway!
  Here is an acronym for FOCUS
  - o **F**ollow **O**ne **C**ourse **U**ntil **S**uccessful
- ➤ Forget Perfection!!! Unless it's a life altering decision there is no need for perfection.

Motivation is a fickle thing. I can disappear for days, weeks, or months and reappear quickly and then disappear again. This is so frustrating. We can't just sit around and wait for motivation to strike or we will not get anything done.

So how do we stay motivated when things get tough?

I've been unmotivated many times in the process of getting my business going and keeping it going. Besides dealing with distractions, life happens. I work a full-time job, I have a husband and bonus daughter, my parents, aunt and my brother, friends and outside interests.

Getting in the mood to work on my business after a long day at work has been my biggest struggle. Somedays I'm just mentally checked out.

Here are a few things that I do to get re-focused and get back or maintain my motivation:

- ➢ Refer to my mission statement because it states my why (Your mission statement should state your why and we all need to have a mission statement both personally and professionally)
- ➢ Look at my goals, dreams, and desires. I have the following question in front of me on my computer.
  - ○ What is the single most important thing that I can do today to move me toward my goal, dream or desire?

Taking a step each day toward your goal keeps you moving along. Baby steps count. Remember to work on one thing at a time.

- ➢ When I review my goals, I ask myself the following:
  - ○ Are these my goals or someone else's?
  - ○ Is this in line with my mission and my current area of focus?

You may be working on a book for instance. What do you want to say and get across to your audience or are you trying to create a book based on what you've seen in the marketplace that has done well?

- ➢ Stay connected to positive people and find a supportive network of other entrepreneurs who are willing to share and uplift each other. This could be locally through a chamber, entrepreneurial center as well as Facebook Groups.

> ➤ I seek out positive information. This can be through affirmations, podcasts, videos, articles, blogs, books, movies, documentaries, etc.

The last thing and one of the most important is:

> ➤ I take time for myself! This is so important and many of us don't do it enough. Self-care is very important and we are all worth it!!!
>> ○ Decide what makes you happy and brings you joy, put yourself on your calendar and go for it!!!

Contact Information:

Robin Robinson Myhand

New Phase of Life

(916) 538-2359

Email: robin@newphaseoflife.com

www.newphaseoflife.com

CHAPTER ELEVEN

Move Forward In Your Purpose

Natasha C. Miller, Author

"Dr. Bill Winston says that we are not here to take sides but to take over and that our assignment is to Advance & Hold!"

As the CEO it is my responsibility to communicate the mission and vision of my organization and my responsibility to be able to have others on my team carry out my mission and vision. My mission is to inspire and motivate moms and women through educating them by obtaining a certification that allows them to make great money working from home, being able to provide for their families and have the option to start their own business. As the CEO, I am the face of my businesses and it important that I protect all of them! Never is it okay for you to let anyone talk badly about your business. As Christian women CEOs, we should never put down our competitors but be lifting up our companies. You must show others how it is a benefit to work with you. As a CEO, I am now learning the importance of working on my business and not just in my business. I am forecasting and looking at what is evolving and what is to come. I also believe in the importance of learning to stay abreast of changes, especially in the healthcare industry. Networking and getting to know other business owners where you can share ideas is another key component to working on your business. Getting out in the community so that people can know that your business exists will also help you in growing your business.

As a CEO you have to continue to learn and grow. Keep up with the changes and stay connected and involved with other CEOs or business owners. There is no reason why a CEO shouldn't be comfortable using a computer and having an understanding of basic computer knowledge. CEOs do not run from problems but face their problems and become change agents by being able to solve their problems. Stay around like-minded people and stay connected to God. All that I have and have become has come from God and all the credit goes to Him! I know that without the Lord I would not be successful and would not be able to help others the way that God graces me to do.

When I see something that will benefit me and my business, I go after it. Many times, I see people get stuck in their thoughts and mind and they never decide to take action. I even see people who say what they are going to do and never do anything. What makes someone go after their dreams and goals is the ability to just move. Growing up I saw my parents were driven and actionable. My parents wanted us to have more than they had so they made sure to provide and give us the best. I remember my father showing us where he grew up in the Projects and how he was grateful for and humble about his beginnings.

An additional quality that I have learned and that I use in my business is that I make a decision. I do not believe in being indecisive. I move and act! The Bible talks about how a double-minded man is unstable in all of his ways. As a Christian woman CEO, you cannot be indecisive. For one, it shows you are not strong in leadership and oftentimes you will have to make uncomfortable decisions.

As a CEO you will sometimes have to make uncomfortable decisions and be in unfamiliar territories. I recently pitched my business to win up to $15,000. Pitching was something I had never done before. I took an entrepreneur program for five months that prepared me to pitch and showed me how to do business better. One thing that I did was practice, practice and practice. My family said to me, "You know your pitch by heart."

I said, "Yes, I want to be comfortable in knowing it, so it doesn't seem like I am just reading the slides."

Of course, I was nervous about standing in front of an audience with unfamiliar faces and having the panel judges right in front of me. God gave me grace to do my pitch and, as a result, I won second place! My business won $10,000! That experience and night of pitching taught me that there is nothing too hard for God to do and He wants to get it to His Kingdom Entrepreneur Citizens to advance His agenda! If God has called you to manage a business or enterprise it will take a lot of work and dedication, and sometimes you will have to decide on things when you may not totally know what to do. It takes using your faith muscle and seeing spiritually.

As a Christian CEO, you should be seeing with your spiritual eye. Have visions of your business and where you see it going. I have visions of my business on a continual basis about where it is going and what it will look like. While writing this chapter the Lord told me to look up the number 12 because I had started my business on 12/12/12 not even realizing the sequence of numbers at the time.

While doing my research I learned that 12 is the symbol of faith, government foundation, a perfect number with God's power and authority (BibleStudy.org, 2019). I didn't realize what that number meant when I started my business, but now that I know the meaning of it I know that God has given me the power and faith to fully continue my race as a CEO!

Being the founder and CEO of Natasha Miller & Associates, LLC., where I have a single company operating multiple businesses—which are Northern California Medical Billing & Coding Institute (NCMBCI), NCM Healthcare, & Natasha C. Miller—takes certain traits that include having faith, staying consistent, believing in the business, having passion, being persistent, and having confidence. All of the traits that I mention do take time to build, but if you work on them daily you will be able to move your business along the upward path of success.

Natasha C. Miller - Medical Mompreneur is my brand where I offer my coaching, speaking, and consulting services, and I am an author and soon will have a podcast. I now as a coach offer my services to help individuals or groups that would like to start or advance their business in healthcare and I show them how they can have clarity and confidence, launch their business, have multiple streams of income and create their products or services. If you are reading this and you have been finding yourself stuck and do not know how to just take action I encourage you to visit my website www.natashacmiller.com and learn about my coaching services. My programs work, and I am helping women all across the world start or advance their businesses. If you are a corporate American CEO and you want to gain clarity and leadership skills, I can also help you in achieving those goals.

All of my businesses are great, but without a plan and strategies I would not be productive. I have to know how to plan, manage, strategize, and implement the businesses' strategies for success. In planning and managing all components I have learned to work on the same tasks across the board for each business. For example, Mondays are my marketing days where I focus on the same tasks for all businesses. You are more productive when you can do the same tasks. Having the role as the founder and CEO in a small business can be a lot at times.

I have learned, and I am learning to be comfortable with knowing my numbers. As a CEO, you have to know your financial numbers. In building an enterprise to be a multi-million-dollar business, and for me to be a multi-millionaire, I have to be comfortable with money and know what is going on with my business financially. Have a financial system in place that tracks your business' gross income, expenses, and net income. I use QuickBooks and it allows me to be able to pull up my monthly profit and loss statement, income statement, yearly reports, and more. Someone recently told me to make Friday mornings about finance for about an hour. It is important for the CEO, entrepreneur, and/or business owner to spend time going over all the financials including sending out any invoices, paying any bills, and planning for the success of your business.

As a CEO, I have learned to build my team! I find myself having many goals that I want to achieve and when I first started my business, I wore all the hats. To not wear all of the hats in a business you have to build a team. As a Christian CEO, you want to learn how to delegate and allow tasks that take away from you making revenue to go to someone else. What I have learned is that if you can map out how you want your business to be once you retire, sell, or maybe transfer your business to your child, then that will help you in the beginning of business. For my business I knew I wanted to have consulting as a part of my business development, but I knew it wasn't going to be possible in the first few years of my business. I developed a plan for how I could eventually incorporate that into my business and now, as a result, consulting is a daily part of my business.

Being a CEO, you have to be able to communicate clearly to your team and to your target audience. Be reliable and provide exceptional service and products. Before I decided to hire a virtual assistant, I knew that I needed to have a clear description of what I wanted her to do. I also knew that I was going to need some visuals to show her on how to do some of the tasks since she would be virtually working in my business. If you are looking to hire a virtual assistant, here is my affiliate link http://store.onlinejobs.ph/?aid=84907 to get you started on finding you the right person to add to your team.

Some tools that I use on a daily basis to help me and my team in being productive, organized, and timely in my businesses are LastPass, Trello, Acuity Scheduling, and SharePoint. LastPass is a password management system that I use every day. LastPass allows me to secure and safeguard my data and passwords. One reason I started using LastPass was because, when I started to build my team, I needed to find a way to conveniently and safely share some of my passwords. LastPass allows me to do that without my team members seeing my passwords. I also control when I want to activate or deactivate someone. Another great feature of LastPass is the vault has within the system the opportunity to sort my websites into folders to make them organized. LastPass also has a secure app that I use on my phone. It comes with a streamlined login, so I do not have to remember all of the passwords that I created for the various websites. LastPass can be used for personal and business purposes.

Trello is a great visual productivity toolkit. It allows me to work with my virtual assistant and keeps things color coordinated and organized. Trello is accessible on my phone via its app and through the website. I have been using this resource for almost three years now and I love it. It allows me to manage my business with my team members. I am able to keep my projects that I work on for all of my businesses within the boards where I can create tasks, due dates, upload attachments and more within the system. Trello is my virtual board where I can say I have this idea, or I would like to have this flyer created and I am able to review and send updates to my virtual assistant or any contractors for revisions. Once I have my final products completed I then move my items to my SharePoint.

SharePoint with Microsoft is another tool that I use on a daily basis. It is a secured internal intranet that allows collaboration and for me to keep all of my policies, procedures, resources, and tools in one place. On SharePoint you can upload presentations, files, folders, and data, and keep everything organized. Since I have multiple businesses with a variety of projects I have to make sure I keep everything organized and easy to find. With my team being contractors, consultants, and part-time employees, I am able to share my resources in and outside of my organization by giving them access to what they need.

Acuity Scheduling is another great tool that I use on a daily basis that allows me and individuals to schedule appointments with me. If I want to charge a fee for an appointment in advance I am able to do that. With Acuity Scheduling you can integrate a variety of apps into the system. For example, I use QuickBooks and anyone who registers for an appointment automatically goes into my QuickBooks. Another awesome integration is that the scheduling system integrates with my Google calendar, so everything automatically pops up on my calendar and I am able to control which days I want my calendar open within the scheduler.

There are many tools and resources to use as an entrepreneur, business owner, or CEO. The key is to find what works for you and your budget and use them. Do not get stuck with trying to use everything that is on the market. Be organized and use what will help you in your business. Keep it simple and use what will help you to grow your business and achieve your goals.

CEOs continue to dream and keep going after your goals and dreams! Also, do not forget to create new goals. Be clear on what your mission and vision is and be able to communicate it. Move and act on decisions, be decisive and put in the work that it takes to move your business forward. One of my favorite scriptures is Philippians 4:13 "I can do all things through Christ, which strengthens me." I live and walk by faith! Woman Christian CEOs continue your journey, advance and hold, move forward and know that your faith is bigger than your fear!

Reference

Biblestudy.org. (2019). Meaning of Numbers in the Bible The Number 12. Retrieved from, https://www.biblestudy.org/bibleref/meaning-of-numbers-in-bible/12.html

Contact Information:

Natasha C. Miller, MS, RHIA, CPC, CPB, CPC-I

CEO, The Medical Mompreneur at NCM Healthcare

(916) 753-8511

Email: natasha@ncmhealthcare.com

www.ncmhealthcare.com

CHAPTER TWELVE

Something about FAITH!

Dr. Dené Starks, Author

"Keep your dreams alive. Understand, to achieve anything requires faith in God, belief in yourself, vision, hard work, determination, and dedication. Remember all things are possible for those who believe."

~ Gail Devers

My Journey Into Entrepreneurship

Like many people, taking the leap into entrepreneurship was not an easy decision for me. I prefer knowing what my paychecks will be every two weeks, what my benefits are, when I will get my bonuses, etc. Working for myself? Why would I do that and stress myself out about a bunch of "unknowns?" I am one of those types of people that will share everything I know with others just to simply help out. My professional mentor always told me "whenever you go higher, you take some people with you." So, every time I would come into some new knowledge or a new opportunity, that's exactly what I tried to do...take some people with me. I was content in doing just that!

I was in corporate America for many years when I realized there had to be more out there. People on the outside would always ask me business questions and I would assist or I would refer them to an appropriate person to assist. After a while, I realized that what I was doing fell under the umbrella of "consulting." After some thought and professional guidance, I decided to launch my first business. I did not know much about setting up a business, so I invested in learning all about it. I invested quite a bit of time and money into getting everything I needed to set up and launch my business. I had so many talents and abilities so why not launch an official business to operate under, gain tax perks, and use a name other than my name.

Now here was the hard part, what do I call it and how much do I charge?

I struggled with the name because I wanted a professional name and I wanted it completely isolated from my name. God has blessed me with lots of business ideas, programs, workshop ideas, class ideas, etc. but I was never a creative person by way of coming up with designs, names, graphics, and the like. On top of that, I had to figure out which services I wanted to offer. Was it going to be a consulting firm, marketing firm, or coaching firm? Was I going to limit my services to what I was best at or was I going to just offer a wide variety of services? Finally, what in the world was I going to charge for these services? After much thought I decided to become a full-service agency and named it DJS Marketing & Business Solutions. This business focused on consulting others and helping them move from the idea stage to the launch stage.

After several years, I prayed and asked God "what's next" for me? After much prayer, I wrote a book called "What's Next: A next level guide for marketing." My book was well supported and I went on to create a workshop based on the book. About eight months after the workshop, in prayer, I heard God say "it's time for your next." I personally did not think I needed to take on anything else because at that time I was in my dissertation stage of school and working full time in the role that I always desired to be in. When God told me to launch my next venture, I simply did not do it. I just felt like I could not do it because I did not have time and I was afraid that I would not have the funding needed to do as God had instructed me. So, guess what...I simply did not do it! As time went on, I had submitted my dissertation for the third time for review and it was rejected. I was completely devastated! All of my time, stress, sacrifices...all of that was a complete waste. I became so angry that I decided to just take a break from school and regroup.

While on a break from school, I took a trip to Massachusetts to speak at a conference. While there God reminded me to launch what he had given me a few months prior. When I returned from Massachusetts, I did exactly what God told me to do. I started a non profit organization called

Diversif-I Education Group, Inc. Although the road to launching was not easy, my delays and dilemmas came during the times when I simply was not trusting God and obeying His word.

When I started the nonprofit, I went to someone who had years of experience in the nonprofit sector to discuss everything I needed to know about nonprofit business, ask questions, and receive guidance. I was immediately told "it will take about 5 years before you will be successful in the nonprofit industry because there's 10,000 nonprofits in Sacramento that do what you do and since you are the new kids on the block no one will ever give you a chance." Hearing these words became very discouraging for me initially. After about a day, I said to myself "God you told me to do this and I trust you!" Just because the path to success for others may have many obstacles, that does not mean that my outcomes will be the same. What did I do? I pressed forward.

Within my first two years, God blessed us to be able to do the following and so much more:

- ✓ Hosted our first conference called "Business & the Bible" in which we exceeded our registration, attendance, and quality targets
- ✓ Hosted workshops and classes on various subjects

- ✓ Networked and presented in front of several community partners
- ✓ Partnered with other nonprofits on several projects
- ✓ Launched a YouTube show and Podcast called "Cross Conversations"
- ✓ Launched a school in Liberia, West Africa
- ✓ Launched a Business degree program

Not only did God meet our expectations, but He EXCEEDED them and we are going full steam ahead with our programs and services.

What is faith?

"Now faith is the substance of things hoped for, the evidence of things not seen."

~ Hebrews 11:1

Faith simply defined is: believing that you have something that does not exist in the physical, sensory, perceptive world that you live in. It does exist in the realm of the spirit but it has not yet manifested in the material world. Faith reaches into the spiritual realm and takes hold of the promise of God's Word and brings it into the realm of reality.

~ Unknown Author

In every aspect of our lives it takes faith to sustain, maintain, and make gains as we moved forward. In business, having faith is a requirement! Without faith, we operate in fear. If we are operating in fear then we are likely not going to reach all of the promises that God has for us.

The lack of faith has many lasting effects!

As Christians, God is our guide and all we have to do is trust Him and follow His plan for our life. The bible declares in Hebrews 11:6, "But without faith *it is* impossible to please *Him*"!

When we lack faith we struggle in our confidence, we struggle in our minds, we never really feel fulfilled, and we often put ourselves in a place of struggle instead of a place of peace.

Fear or Faith...You choose!

One thing about me, I am a risk taker. If someone said "don't do it" ...I would do it anyway. If someone said "this is dangerous, scary, or risky" ... I would try it out to see if it was actually dangerous, scary, or risky. Sometimes my experience would line up with what "they" said and other times it would not. Either way, about 90% of the time I was going to take the risk. I tell people all the time "you'll never know if you don't try." Unfortunately, so many people...don't try! Many of us have goals, dreams, aspirations, and desires that oftentimes lay dormant because for whatever reason many people WILL NOT take the risk.

Statistics show that 80% of people in America will spend the majority of their lifetime working for someone else. The top reason that people do not take risks (even small ones) is FEAR. People naturally fear the unknown. Can you relate to any of these?

1. Believing your idea is worthless

Many people do not take the risk because they do not believe that their idea is worth it. Some people think like this "there's 1 million books in the world, why should I write my story when someone else has already talked about what I would talk about?"

Guess what? When you go to the grocery store to purchase bread you will see multiple options for bread. Does that stop the bread maker from making another loaf? NO!

Overcome this fear by understanding that your idea is unique and meets the needs of an untapped market.

2. Lack of confidence in yourself

Many people have been told "you'll never do this or do that," "you'll never be this or be that."

The problem with believing in this ideology is that if you allow the labels that people put on you to deter you then you stay stagnant while their life goes on! Ask yourself, do I want to live in fear or move forward in the abundance of what God has for me?

3. Afraid to be successful

"What will people say if I am successful?" "What if I make a lot of money?" "What if people talk trash about me because I am successful?"

We often worry ourselves about things that just do not matter. WHO CARES about "them?" Fearing success is a negative mindset that will keep you stagnant. You have to learn to plan for success instead of being fearful of success.

4. Inadequate Resources

Launching out in business, providing services, starting a ministry, etc....MONEY IS REQUIRED!

The old saying "It takes money to make money" is a very true statement. Many people do not launch out because they do not have the capital, they "think" they need to get started.

In reality, depending on the business or idea, a lot of up-front capital may not be necessary. There are several things that can be done to ensure proper planning so that the launch is seamless.

a. Speak to a business consultant.

It is important to consult your ideas with the right person that can lead and guide you in an upward direction. Most business ideas never launch or do not last more than 5 years simply due to lack of knowledge.

b. Create a business plan.

Planning for success is key. Business gurus always say "without a plan, you plan to fail." The Bible says "write the vision, make it plain" ...Habakkuk 2:2.

c. Pace yourself!

Remember, you do not have to do everything at one time. Set short-term and long-term goals with achievable targets.

5. Lack of Faith

Many people, believers and non-believers alike, lack in their faith. Lacking faith causes blockage in many areas of a person's life. Most will only go so far because they lack in their faith. If you're going to launch in business...you MUST HAVE FAITH!

Conclusion

Do you want to be a part of the 80% who will always work for someone else, build someone else's dreams, or help someone else reach their goals? Are you tired of feeling unfulfilled? Are you tired of forfeiting your own goals for the sake of someone else?

If this is you...take the leap of faith and become ALL that God wants you to be. Just try it! Know that he has you right in the palm of His hand. If He said it, it will come to pass. All you have to do is listen for His leading and GO!

Contact Information:
Dr. Dené Starks
Diversif-I Education Group, Inc.
(916) 542-2679
Email: team@diversifieducationgroup.org

CHAPTER THIRTEEN

Empowerment Coach on the Move

Kyna Kemp, Author

Are you looking for career advancement? Do you need an accountability partner? Do you struggle with organization or time management? Are you ready to reach your goals? If you answered yes to any of these questions, I am here to help you.

My name is Kyna Kemp and I am an author, coach, mentor, speaker, and teacher. I also hold a full-time job, as well as being a wife to my loving husband and a mother to two wonderful sons.

As an Empowerment Coach, I specialize in the areas of Career Advancement, Goal Setting, Organization, Personal Development, and Time Management. My goal is to empower individuals to reach their goals, identify and work through the fears and obstacles keeping them from being successful. My experience spans from years of leadership roles in Corporate America, which has allowed me to pour into the lives of all that I come in contact with. My daily tasks include: creating and monitoring performance goals and measures, motivating staff to reach their goals, identifying roadblocks, holding staff accountable, determining adequate staffing requirements and resources are available and developing staff to maximize their potential. Being in a leadership role can be rewarding as well as demanding.

Working with staff over years, I have noticed there were two problem areas I was constantly addressing: Organization and Time Management. While networking with other leaders, it was revealed that these two areas were also being addressed in other workplaces. I decided to create an organization plan and time management schedule to assist staff with meeting their performance expectations. Although staff were reluctant to use the new processes, their performance rates began to rise. Sharing the results with staff, allowed me to encourage and empower them to meet their performance measures each week and strive to reach higher measures. As a result of the success, I continue to use the plan on a daily basis and have turned each into six-week coaching programs. The strategies and tools provided in each coaching program will allow individuals to become more organized and develop effective time management habits in order to be more productive and successful in every area of life.

Let me share how I show up and make a difference in the lives of the individuals I work with. I promoted earlier this year and on my last day my former staff shared how much they were going to miss me, my personality, laughter and leadership style. There was one message from a former staff who I coached and mentored as an analyst, which really spoke to my leadership skills and abilities. I am excited to share this testimonial.

I have known Kyna Kemp for over five years as employees of the State of California. Kyna originally started with the department as the Staff Services Manager 1 for Reporting Unit 1. In 2016, she became the manager of my unit in Reporting Unit 2.

Shortly after Kyna became my manager, she promoted me into a Staff Services Analyst vacancy. Despite my hesitancy in the position, Kyna helped foster my leadership skills and encouraged my personal growth. Despite being unsure of my abilities, Kyna helped change my outlook and helped me reach my potential as an analyst. She showed immense leadership ability. Whenever I had doubts or needed guidance, Kyna was there for me.

By having someone like Kyna to confide in, she helped by encouraging me and keeping me motivated to strive for the best job I could do. She would add responsibilities to allow me to grow in my career, without inundating me. Kyna allowed me to find the solution to a problem, by not always taking the "standard" path. If I could find the solution (with a slightly different path and same end results), Kyna approved.

One of my favorite quotes by Kyna (of which I still have hanging at my desk) is "Is it fixable?" She had faith I could handle the problem and find the solution. Most often, she was correct. Kyna is a remarkable leader with great vision. She finds strength in her employees and she listens. She is a rare, shining example of a true leader.

CHALLENGES

As a business owner, challenges are bound to surface. The two biggest challenges I faced were fear and lack of marketing.

Fear

What is fear? Fear is False Evidence Appearing Real.

I had a hard time starting my Coaching Business. I took the certification class in October 2017, but did not start thinking about putting my program together until mid-2018. Every time I started to work on my program, negative thoughts would begin my mind:

There are so many Empowerment Coaches in the marketplace, why are you starting a coaching business?

How is your program different from other programs already in existence?

147

What do you have to offer people?

Why would people choose your program?

What qualifies you to be a coach?

As a result, fear had set in and literally paralyzed me from wanting to start my own business. I was afraid of:

1. **Failure** – I'm the type of person where everything has to be perfect, otherwise I don't want to do it. I don't like to fail. Starting a business brings about the fear not knowing if you are going to succeed.

2. **What people will say or think** – Sometimes words from family/friends can be hurtful or discouraging. If you dwell on the words long enough, they began to feel like sharp punches. I had to realize, no matter what I do, someone will always have something to say, positive or negative.

One day I had enough of the negative self-talk. I began to seek God for direction. I began to quote powerful scriptures and positive affirmations each morning.

II Timothy 1:7 (NKJV) – For God has not given us the spirit of fear, but of power and of love and of a sound mind.

Psalms 139:14 (NKJV) - *I will praise You, for I am fearfully and wonderfully made; Marvelous are Your works, And that my soul knows very well.*

Proverbs 18:21 (NKJV) – *Death and life are in the power of the tongue, and those who love it will eat its fruits.*

Philippians 4:13 (NKJV) – *I can do all things through Christ who strengthens me.*

As the days went by, God allowed me to see what I needed to do. One morning, God simply asked, "Kyna, what are you afraid of? You are a leader. Every day you pour into the lives of your staff and the young adults you work with. You have helped people set and achieve their goals, promote in their careers, meet deadlines, become clear on their vision, and identified problem areas and solutions. You've got what it takes. Just believe in yourself, as I do. Someone needs to hear what you have to say, so be the voice the world needs."

This message was also confirmed when one of my staff gave me a gift. It was a coffee mug which says, "Be the voice the world needs".

I no longer allow fear to keep me from doing what God has called me to do and I am moving forward in my purpose.

Advertising/Marketing

I did not utilize all the marketing strategies for promoting my business. At that time, I was thinking on a small scale, so the options I used for advertising were:

- Business
- Postcards
- Attending networking events
- Speaking events
- Word of Mouth

This sparked some traffic, however, not the revenue producing business I had hoped. I realized I started to just utilize options that I had seen other businesses use, I had not created an actual marketing plan or strategy. I needed to determine what my business would look like, identify my target audience and engage in social media networks. Again, fear set in because this was an area that I was unfamiliar with and did not know how to really get started. I had to push past the fears, and now I am in the process of revamping my website, getting clear on my ideal audience, creating a brand and will identify which social media networks to utilize in order to really market my business.

TIPS TO OVERCOME CHALLENGES

As Christian Women CEO's our best resource is God. If and when you face any type of challenges, seek God first for direction and guidance. Consult with God on every move/decision you make.

Own who you are and it will always come off as authentic. Be open to operating outside of the box.

Stay true to yourself. Conduct and run your business the way God's gives it you. There may be several different businesses that offer the same services you do, but someone is waiting for your business.

Don't allow fear to paralyze you from doing what God has called you to do. Trust God and he will provide all the resources you need. Be patient and trust the process that God had for you.

Don't share your dreams with everyone. Some people will not agree or see your vision as you do and will try to persuade you in a different direction or discourage you altogether.

Have a mentor or business coach – for sound advice, creative and new ways to present your business. No need to make unnecessary mistakes, if you don't have to.

When times get hard, don't give up. Stay the course and you will succeed.

If you are looking for a good book to read:

The 21 Laws Irrefutable Laws of Leadership

by John C. Maxwell

Contact Information:

Kyna Kemp

Empowerment Coach

Email: CoachKyna18@gmail.com

Website: www.kynakemp.com

Business Number: (916) 572-7332

CHAPTER FOURTEEN

**To Whom Much Is Given,
Much Will Be Required
Luke 12:48**

Dr. Kathy James, Author

To Whom Much Is Given, Much Will Be Required

Luke 12:48

If you have heard this line of wisdom, you know it means we are held responsible for what we have. If we have been blessed with talents, wealth, knowledge, time, and the like, it is expected that we benefit others.

Do you want to be a successful CEO Woman? Of course, you do. We all want that. Most of us strive for happy, successful lives.

However, what success means to each of us is a unique and individual thing, based on our specific desires and goals. It also changes over time for each of us. Your professional goals and measures for success at the beginning of your journey will probably look different than when you're older and further along in your journey. I am sharing with you some CEO musts to help bring awareness to you along the path that God has breathed into you as you journey to success to benefit the world.

I Can, I Will, I Am Able

When I turned 50 years of age, I completed a 26.3-mile marathon in Kauai Hawaii. I trained with a group of 100 individuals who were committed and determined to participate and successfully complete a sports event that only 3-5% of the world's population can declare I did it. The team had a mantra that we quoted often and we encouraged each member of our team. Simply said, I Can, I Will, I Am Able. Do you believe that you Can? Do you believe that you Will, and do you believe that you are Able to be a Chief Executive Officer (CEO)?

I ran a 26.3-mile marathon. I did it! This event has always resonated in the recesses of my mind as a great accomplishment. I trained faithfully to run the marathon in 5.0 hours it took me 6.0 long grueling hours. There were many unexpected feelings and emotions along my journey and I can't begin to tell you the pain that I endured along the way but in the end, I can declare that I am a Marathoner. It would be unfair to not mention that along this journey I met some amazing people. The team members became a part of my life and shared and cried with me all the way. The team supported me when I could not support myself.

The last .3 miles I ran with team members who circled back to run with me after they had finished their race, and received their medals to get me. They wanted to make sure that I finished my race too. **A CEO must** know how to stay in the race (help is on the way). Faithfully training, committed, and have an I don't quit spirit, it pays off.

In order to be successful marathoner, there was a lot of preparation (training) that had to be done. I had to commit to multiple regular weekly trainings that required me to build my muscle strength, my body core, and to run anywhere from 3 to 20-mile sessions weekly and logging 50-70 miles per week until the big day. I was determined to train and progress along with my teammates on the journey of success.

I learned some valuable lessons on this journey of completing a marathon. As a CEO there are many life lessons that you must know how to effectively use to be successful. You must know <u>when</u> and <u>how</u> to use the lessons to your advantage in the right moment to propel you into your destiny. Actually, you must know how and when to use them in your favor for success.

<u>What A CEO Must Know</u>

A CEO must know that running a company is like a running a marathon you cannot do it from a thought to an action item and come out uninjured. A true alethic knows that it takes consistent training (running) to be a marathoner. A marathoner must manage a grueling schedule around their personal and work life for the "I did it". A successful CEO must be as diligent and committed as a marathoner. A successful business will not "just" appear.

A CEO must realize the commitment involved in saying I am a life coach, a leader, a speaker, a hands-on expert whatever you name your life calling. The people you service are trusting you and your expertise. Make sure that you get it right.

A CEO must know that running a marathon is a team event. You cannot do this alone you need a team. You need a cheer section and cheerleaders, people who believe in you. You don't need a lot of people on the team; you just need your team.

A CEO must know that running a marathon is against all odds, your body fights back (I don't like this). There will be times that you doubt yourself and your abilities to be great at your life calling. When you stare in the face all the skills and knowledge that are required to be a successful CEO fear can grip you. You must find the courage to speak your God given talents and gifts into the world that you know possess. Don't allow your thoughts to overtake and play games with your mind. Remember Proverbs 23:7 "As a woman thinks so she becomes". Place your feet on the ground and take your rightful place.

A CEO must know that running a marathon is going to you push you beyond your own minds ability to see the finish line. During your run there will be times that you must bare down with your whole heart and soul, give it all you got. You have read the banners "Bust or Go home". When you get tired, when the pain begins to become unbearable, when you feel that first blister you have to push. A CEO has to push their dream into existence. I am not going home without a win.

A CEO must know the power of the mind. The brain is the most powerful muscle in the body. You must learn to trust it and to nourish it wholeheartedly. You must believe in yourself. When the lights go out at night you must speak to your brain, tomorrow is another day and I will get up and I will start again. It is true that the body will follow the brain. With that said - Brain let's get it done.

Responsibility

♦ Responsibility is the opportunity or ability to act independently and make decisions without authorization.

A CEO must know the responsibilities involved in running a company. Your clients have entrusted their lives and resources into your expert skills, knowledge and abilities. That is a frightening feeling and an awesome responsibility don't let them down. Learn to make informed decisions and take responsibility for every step you make. Own everything that you have been empowered to implement.

I am a successful business owner. I do not believe in failure. I believe in doing it again another way. I had to learn how to keep my mind clear so that I could hear the voice of success. **A CEO must** remind yourself constantly that success cries out "**hard work**" ahead to reach your goal. Success requires specialty workout shoes and clothes so that you can feel equipped for the job. Do you have the right gear?

Trust The Bread Crumbs

Sometimes you can feel lost on this journey of living your best life to get to success. But if you take the time to look deeply within, you will find breadcrumbs. Breadcrumbs are the steps that will guide you to your success. Many others have paved the way and suffered many trails to reach their success, follow their breadcrumbs. When you follow the breadcrumbs, you can avoid the many unnecessary mistakes that others have made along the way, and paid the horrible price of starting over. A smart diligent CEO would do well to study and travel the path of the behaviors of their hero's in the business world.

Permission To Ask

On the journey to your success give yourself permission to ask the hard questions. When you face difficulties on you journey don't hesitate to ask questions. Asking the questions will remind you why you are on this specific journey.

If you fail to ask yourself the questions and life goes unfulfilled on your business journey you will be more than disappointed and you will feel like a failure. You should also ask questions of your business partners, your peers and of people that you trust. Be a wise Stewart and look closely behind the why others failed and take notes.

Read the Headlines

Today we are fortunate entrepreneurs there is so much information available for us to read and study. The why's and the how's have already been answered. As a **CEO you must** do the work of being strategic and methodical in your processes. There is no need to waste time and money trying to figure things out. Read the headlines. The best strategies are found in seeking and reading God's Word daily, and being prayerful for your success on the CEO trail.

Proven Success Tips

- Make a solid plan.

- Transform your mind to believe that you can.

- Enforce boundaries for yourself and others to respect.

- Commit yourself fully to the success journey.

- Learn the power of effective communication.

- Maintain strong connections with yourself and your peers.

In life you have the people who are out there living it to the fullest and the bystanders letting it pass them by. You have the people who sit around and mope all day about how miserable their lives are, then you have the people who are out there crossing things off their bucket lists on a regular basis. You.

In business, you have the people who started from nothing and didn't do anything to change their situations, like the people born rich. Then you have the people who saw whatever little opportunity they had and make the most of it. You.

Success is more than an idea; it is a state of mind. Although success is relative to each individual, the key to achieving success is the demeanor and attitude in which you go about living your life and taking advantage of opportunities that come to you.

Whether it is in life or in business, you should never take anything for granted and you should learn how to make the most of the situations that are presented to you.

Trust The Process

- Learn to listen to your gut feeling.
- Have an open mind when it comes to unfamiliar ways of thinking.
- Accept new technologies and try to learn as much about them as you can.
- Constantly educate yourself.
- Give back when you can.
- Be street smart as well as book smart.
- Care for yourself.
- Treat others with respect.

Anything that you want to achieve is going to take time and, most importantly, effort. Time is your most valuable asset and if you are truly invested in something, your efforts and time will be all you have to offer. That is why it is important that you choose a business goal that you really enjoy because you must be committed to it.

Nothing comes easy in this world and if you really want something, then you are going to stop at nothing to make it happen. If you find yourself losing interest in particular business goal, then it was never meant to be. Finding your passion may be the most difficult part of your life, but once you find it, you will stop at nothing to make your dreams come true.

I invite you to join me at the table the feast has been spread and the King awaits your arrival.

I Can, I Will, I Am Able

A CEO WOMAN

Contact Information:
Dr. Kathy A. James, CEO
Esthernation Ministries &
Crosswalk Life Coaching and Consulting
(916) 549-9363
Esternationministries.org

CHAPTER FIFTEEN

Inner Beauty ABC's for Business

Carla Preyer, Author

ATTITUDE

Your **Attitude** towards the calling on your life is probably one of the most important tools for success in business. I remember when the previous owner of the salon I had worked in for 7 years decided to semi-retire, leaving me to take over the salon. Although I had always said I wanted to own my own salon, I didn't think I was ready at that point, but I decided to put on my big girl pants and change my attitude from fearful to fearless. Everything I needed for a successful business was already inside me. At that point, I decided to either take the necessary classes in the areas where I was weak or simply hire someone for those areas, as needed.

In the classes I took, I learned how important it was to have a clear picture of how you want to introduce yourself to the world, which is your Brand. Your Brand is like your bond. What are people saying about you and your business when they leave? Often, people tell me they feel like I care because I take time to listen. I heard Oprah Winfrey say that a person may not remember what you said but they will remember how you made them feel.

CHANGE

Change is necessary and inevitable. Change will take place, with or without your permission. In order to stay in business, you have to be willing to keep up with the times. For example, when I started doing hair in the early 1980s, beauty salons did not use computers in operating their businesses. Now, I can't imagine doing business without a computer. What about the application of hair color? Back in the early 1980s, we used tint bottles. Now, I only use tint bottles to administer scalp treatments. One of the latest things I had to change was my attitude about natural hair. When I first got into the business, it was all about chemical relaxers. Because I want to maintain my clientele, I had to change and embrace natural hair. I must say that I have come to love nurturing our many curls and textures. It is very important to know when to change a service, employees, or the actual physical location of your business.

When you are in a relationship with your Creator, you will hear His voice on the small and big issues. Life has a way of presenting obstacles. The obstacles make you stronger and/or help redirect your path. Just a little over a year ago, I had an appointment to get my hair cut by one of my colleagues in downtown Sacramento. But I kept feeling this pull to go see another barber who I hadn't seen in a while. I went back and forth several times, trying to decide which barber to go to, and I could not shake the pull to go see the barber who I hadn't seen in a while. Finally, I called Dominick to let him know I was having trouble getting into his website and I needed to make an appointment with him to get my hair cut.

As he was cutting my hair, I was sharing with him that if I ever decided to close my salon... but before I could finish my sentence he belted out "I BETTER BE YOUR FIRST CHOICE!!!" After putting my heart back in my chest from the fear of him yelling at me, while still shaking, I whispered to him that his shop was my only choice. LOL. In the middle of getting my hair cut, Dominick took me to this two-station room in the back of his shop. This space was just enough room for me. Within four months I closed my former location and moved my business to Dominick's shop. This was one of the many times I've heard God's small, soft voice and I acted on it. I am s-o-o-o amazed at how He knew what I needed before I realized what I needed. I must say, that was the best move for me. But keep in mind, I had to be willing to hear the voice of God and change my location.

DELIVER

It is important that you **Deliver** spiritually, mentally, physically and emotionally while delivering your service. I've made it my goal to always give my best in my business, with my clients and co-workers. When you deliver your best, it releases any self-doubt, because you have given your all.

EDUCATION

Education is not an option. Although I never went to business school, I've always taken classes every chance I could. A situation came up that led to my business being audited by the Board of Equalization. With my heart pounding, I went into my first appointment at the Board of Equalization, not knowing what to expect. I gave the auditor all of my paperwork. She looked puzzled and asked me how many employees I had. I told her I've always only had one employee at a time. The puzzled look on her face concerned me, at first. She spoke with another person in the office and she also had that puzzled look on her face. They told me it is very rare for a business as small as mine to get audited. The auditor said she would get back to me. I waited a couple of weeks, on pins and needles and worried sick about the possible outcome. Ms. Auditor called me and asked "Carla, are you sitting down?" I gulped and fearfully said "yes." She said "I've gone through your files and with all of your fines and penalties the amount you owe is...... (long pause) .... $27.23." Hmmmm.... Who knew I would end up with a comedian for an auditor?? It turned out that someone reported me because I had to make the necessary changes for the health and reputation of my salon. Oh, no need to feel sorry for me, the story turned out okay. I told Ms. Auditor I did not have a business degree and wanted to know how I was doing in business. Again, she had this puzzled look on her face and said "You don't have a degree???" I replied "No, I have just taken classes at different hair shows and business classes here in town." Ms. Auditor said "Carla, you are doing business better than many other people that have been in business for over 20 years, with a degree." You see, what was meant for harm turned out for my good and left me feeling pretty intelligent, if I must say so myself

FOCUSED & GRATEFUL

When you operate in your calling it makes it easy to stay **Focused**. This is not to say life won't have its challenges and distractions. When this happens, be prepared to have a laser focus. This will minimize the distractions.

Gratitude goes along way. Everyone wants to feel appreciated. A simple thank you goes farther than you think. Something as simple as giving a holiday thank you gift at the end of the year can leave a lasting impression. Clients have told me they still have Christmas gifts I gave them 10 years ago. Being a healthy you, both spiritually, mentally and physically is so important. There have been times when I did not pace myself in those areas. I was not getting proper sleep. I ate poorly over a period of time and failed to exercise. I kept putting off drinking my water. My creativity was off. I was not my upbeat, joyful self, which was a sign that all of my spark plugs were not firing in harmony. Then, one day my body just crashed, forcing me to cancel all my clients and I was down for a few days. This is not the way to treat the temple God has blessed me with or to be an example for others.

Integrity can make you or break you. Doing the right thing, for the right reason is always the right choice. Integrity takes you on a path where you will never get lost.

JOY, UNSPEAKABLE JOY

The **Joy** of the Lord helps me smile when others don't understand how I'm able to smile. I have had major events hit left and right in my life in a fairly short period of time. These are the times where you can let the world see how having God in your life will carry you through the storm. Have you ever been around someone who just complains about everything? They complain about health, family, relationships, money and other things. These are joy vampires. I'm exhausted just typing these words down! Joy is a simple choice. I choose to create and keep a joyful atmosphere so that I can stay in a business where clients enjoy coming. I know this, because I get a lot of feedback on how my clients feel when they come into my establishment.

REMAINING RELEAVANT

Keeping up with your craft and technology is a must because times are continually changing. I truly believe that's the reason for my longevity in business comes from many of the ABC's I have listed earlier: Attitude, Brand, Change, Delivery, Education, Focus, Gratitude, Health, Integrity, Joyfulness and Keeping up.

If you don't have the Motivation, you may not be in the right field, or you may need to look at what's motivating you to go into a particular field. Take the time to do some soul searching to see what's motivating you. You may need to make some minor decisions that will make all the difference in the world.

Just like raising a child, you have to **Nurture** your business. Feeding your child/business, with the right foods/tools allow optimum growth. Spending time with that child/business will cause it to go in the direction you desire.

I had to be **Open** for new possibilities and ideas. So long as the idea fits under the umbrella of the overall wealth and health of the business of hair, skin and nails, Some of the products I have incorporated over time are IMPAX herbal products, Nature Sunshine Herbal products, Flow Hair Growth Industries and CTFO.

PUNCUTAL & RESPECTFUL

Back in the day, I worked in a salon where it was the hangout. But as I matured in business, I realized that if I wanted to maintain and keep my professional clientele, I needed to be **Punctual** and **Respectful** of their time by getting the clients in and out in a timely manner. At the same time, I make sure I am providing Quality service in a Relaxed atmosphere.

The Beauty of my business is that I get to be Spontaneous, which can be an adventure in itself. I laugh when my clients have an appointment for one thing and because of some change in their lives, or they are bored and just want something different. They come in and decide they want a completely different look, style, and color. If time permits, I have to be ready to go with the flow.

Having **Trust** is a big factor, whether it is personal or professional. On a professional level, my clients know I am about strong, healthy hair and they trust that I'm getting the education I need to provide them with quality service and the products they need. On a personal level, I cannot count the times clients have confided in me about something and regardless of how intertwined I am in their lives, they know that no matter what they have shared with me, the conversation stays right in that chair.

CONCLUSION

My goal in business is for a client to leave my presence feeling safe, secure and **Uplifted**. With all of the negativity floating around the world today, I am always looking for ways to uplift myself and others.

When you come to Inner Beauty Hair Design you will find inspirational books, music, and quotes around the salon. This is a must for me, at the salon and at home.

When you show your clients, you care and are transparent, they feel **Valued**. I have heard of some businesses where the employee or operator was on the phone, talking with everyone except to the client in the chair. The client does not feel **Welcomed**. What about being your own walking "welcome" sign? A polite "Hello. How's your day?" shows your clients they are truly welcomed.

In the Cambridge Dictionary, a quality that you cannot describe that makes someone very special is the definition of the **X Factor**. What's your X Factor? What are your clients saying about you when they leave your business?

Your willingness to say Yes to the call God has placed in your heart and business makes a great impact on the **Zeal** you have and shows up in your dedication and enthusiasm for your business. If you have Zeal, you're willing, energized, and motivated to take on the task at hand.

My mantra is:
"I Can Do All Things Through Christ Who Strengthens Me"
(Philippians 4:13)

Contact Information:
Carla Preyer
(916) 501-8612
Email: innerbeautybycarla@gmail.com

CHAPTER SIXTEEN

Birthing While You are Working

Coach Charlene Johnson, Author

One of the most beautiful events in a woman's life is the ability to give life to another human being. Conceiving, carrying, nurturing, and delivering a precious human soul into the earth realm is one of the most miraculous events ever known to mankind. Although we have gained much research regarding the intricate, detailed, design of the human body, still the human being remains a mystery because of its complex relationship between the body, soul, and spirit. I believe that every human being is a walking miracle traveling through space and time created to impact others' lives on a journey to a destination here on earth. One moment in time can alter your entire destiny in a flash--just by embracing and being open to it. This chapter is an example of one miraculous moment that totally altered lives that would not have normally been touched, if this moment had not occurred. The word "miracle" according to Webster's dictionary, is "an effect or extraordinary event in the physical world that surpasses all known human or natural powers and is ascribed to a supernatural cause a remarkable event or thing." Miracles are not promised, but they happen all the time and we can receive so much from a miracle if we can "see" or grasp it.

My favorite nursing theorist, Jean Watson, explains that

the Latin word "Theoria" means "to see," so my job in this chapter is to help you to see one of the most wonderful miracles that has ever manifested in my life while I was at work. My prayer is that you would be inspired to the point that you will begin to recognize all the many miracles that happen that you would have normally not recognized, had you not read this chapter. My task also for this book is to cause you to recognize that you are more than your occupation. You are a moving body of love and compassion and you have a power that can create love and healing and release miracles into the earth realm just by simply caring and being who God ordained you to be.

Count Your Blessing

I have been a registered nurse for 26 years; the last 10 of those a Nurse Leader. It has been one of the most rewarding jobs filled with so many daily blessings. When God gives us a dream, vision, or idea it takes a process to birth. If you ask most people who they are, they would probably say; "I am a nurse, I am a doctor, or I am a secretary," but notice the question is not what do you do? The question is who you are? This was a powerful distinction because I was working but began to experience unrest right in the center of my gut. Although I was successful, working, making a great salary, something deep within me was longing for something more. I began to recognize that although nursing is what I do, it is not who I am. It is part of my journey that allows me to make a difference in people's lives, but my Manufacturer was calling me to do more. It is my occupation, not my vocation so there was this restlessness within me that I wrestled to figure out how to merge who I am with what I do. Can you understand that phrase?

Does what you do line up with who you are? In my case, my job matches my make-up thus becoming a vehicle that God is using for my transformation and elevation. However, for many people their occupation does not match their vocation thereby producing frustration, stagnancy, and unrest.

Instead of recognizing this and counting my blessings, I allowed my frustration, grumbling, and complaining to make me blind to what God was doing. I was in my process and it was making me uncomfortable, so I decided to complain about it. God spoke and said, *"Daughter, why are you complaining? You are blessed! Count your blessings, open your eyes, and you will see why I have you here.* I immediately stopped complaining. My job was a gift that He blessed me with as part of my process and life journey. I had an organization that believed in excellence, quality, and leadership. I was encouraged to upgrade my leadership skills and knowledge with free training. "Wake up! Charlene, you are inspiring people to become the best version of themselves right here at work." I immediately repented because I had gotten so consumed with the fact that I was so tired of working that my eyes became dim. I wanted to just quit, jump out on faith, (or should I say foolishness) and birth my dream. The very thing that I needed to help me become the best version of myself was the very thing that I was trying to run away from. Lord, help us to see how You see!

How many of you complain and get so frustrated about the job that you have asked God for? Stop complaining and count your blessings. Look around you and see the silver lining. Look around and see who God is using to sharpen you...to push you...to teach you! You are in the process every day and you need to be ok with that. During this process, He uses people and our situations to love harder, to forgive quicker, to yield more, to innovate solutions, and to dream more. If we keep running from the process, we will never become that brilliant diamond that he is trying to create us into.

The Miracle at Work

As we leave our homes for our places of

employment, we never think twice about the impact that we will make in someone's life or the impact that will be made in our lives as we venture out to complete our usual daily routine. Well 8 years ago, I never imagined that when I left my house I would be invited into the most spectacular miracle of my life.

As a manager, normally I wear business clothes. This particular night when I stepped on the unit, I felt chaos and busyness, so I decided to just put on my scrubs as soon as I got there. A few hours later I found myself in the most intense resuscitation (and miracle) I had experienced in my 17-year career. Around 3am, I hear on the overhead, Code-C—Labor and Delivery, Code C—Labor and Delivery (a life-threatening emergency is taking place rapidly). We rush a mom back to the operating room because her baby is in trouble, we deliver this pale, limp, frail baby that came out with no life in him at all. I am thinking, No worries! This is what we do! WE got this! As we all jump into action resuscitating and trying to hear a heart rate, a flicker of hope, or anything— five minutes passed—no heart beat—no breathing, 10 minutes passed no heart rate— no breathing, 15 minutes passed, Oh my God! This can't be— no heart rate—no breathing—a couple more minutes after that we all looked at one another and knew that we had done all that we could do. The tears began to stream down our cheeks. "This can't be happening!" I thought. The doctor said, "Let's stop!" We were all devastated. "Wait a minute; we are supposed to help bring life!" Everyone in the room began to cry it seemed in one voice without even making a sound. As I stood by, the different team members began to leave, I remember looking at the mother with her eyes closed, unconscious, having no idea that we had lost her little precious baby.

I was so broken up with compassion in my heart—but I could feel the prayers in the room, I felt the need to touch the little limp angel and speak life into him silently, so I held his little hand, which felt like an ice cube and said softly, "*God grant this family a miracle!*" I moved out of the way and stood there as I watched the doctor reluctantly take the breathing tube out. The little angel was wrapped up and place by his side so that when mom woke up, she would be able to meet him and then say goodbye to her little angel. We all were traumatized with tears in our eyes as we pressed in to finish the surgery—boy! It was so hard to continue—there was a painful silence in the room--you could hear a pin drop.

At about 17 minutes, the doctor said, "*I am going to listen one more time!*" He listens, "Hey there's a faint heart rate!" I thought, "Oh my God!" I quickly grabbed the baby, zoomed to the nursey and we began life sustaining measures again. As I put him on the monitor, we see a heart rate! Oh, what joy that erupted in that room! I yelled, "Thank You Jesus!" Could he have come back to us? Yes, he came back to us! This little angel declared that he had a purpose bigger than life and he wanted to fulfill it! This night at work will go down as a miracle. He was sent home within 2 weeks after his birth! Wow! What a moment—birthing while I am working! Paul said in Philippians 3:12; "Not *that I have already obtained all this, or have already arrived at my goal, but I press on to take hold of that for which Christ Jesus took hold of me.*" He was saying, I will not stop until I lay hold of what God has laid hold of me for. That's the type of tenacity you must have if you are to birth your dream while you are working. The vision in my heart is so much bigger than my circumstances, so that keeps me going. As I look back at this miracle, I ponder, what if I had quit! What would have been the outcome.

How to Hold onto your Dream when you are working a 9-5 job?

If money was no object, you would be pursuing your dream, right? If you are employed right now, I encourage you to continue to stay put and put feet to your faith and continue to hold onto your dream—be ok with where you are right now but never satisfied. The worst thing you can do in this moment is to get frustrated and become bitter with where you are on your journey. God wants to use you to represent His brand down here on this earth while you are pursuing your dream. Let patience have its perfect work and find you doing the work necessary to create the life that you want. What are you doing with your free moments? Are you letting other people's emergencies become your emergencies? Are you working on things that have nothing to do with your purpose?

To successfully balance the two, self-development and transformation is critical. We must master our moments and do the personal work required so that we can become a master of our emotions. I recently found this quote, *"Maybe the journey isn't so much about becoming as it is unbecoming everything that isn't really you so that you can be who you were meant to be in the first place" Paulo Coelho.* Unbecoming everything that is not like you—what a statement! Many of us cannot even start the journey because we still have the remnants of the past imbedded in us which is causing us to be someone that we truly are not. The people we trusted, the words spoken and unspoken, that we embraced as truth are all things we internalize until they shape us into who we are. Unbecoming takes a process because of the people we fashioned ourselves after that truly didn't serve us well. You must purge any and everything that is not the real you because the Real You is who we become after this journey— Not the you that you lost in other people. Not the one that you have been told you are, not the one that you have become because of needing someone to love you, or the one that placed unrealistic expectations on you. I encourage you as you are working, unbecome all those things that don't serve you.

Developing Resilience

Besides counting your blessings, it is critical that you develop resiliency in your life. The popular definition of resilience is "to bounce back from setbacks." The Heart Math definition of resilience is "the capacity to prepare for, recover from, and to adapt in the face of stress,

challenge, or adversity." There are 3 parts to this definition because in the times we live in, you will have to learn that resilience is a daily practice, so you must build your resiliency muscle by leaning into the challenges of life. Recovering from those setbacks that tend to knock the breath out of us is important as well. You not only want to bounce back, but you want to bounce back stronger. Adapting in the face of challenges causes you to be a stronger person, that begins to shine like a diamond. I no longer see "problems", I see opportunities for me to become better and innovate my way out of situations. In a way, I am leaning into the challenge which causes my brain to start reinventing itself by listening to the Holy Spirit as He gives answers.

How do you respond to extreme setbacks?

There are a few ways that people respond to extreme setbacks. The first one is to implode, meaning when challenges come, you go internally, get numb, get quiet, lose power, and you shut off from the world. Others explode when the assault hits, they blow off the handle, get upset, and angry. Then there are the resilient ones that get hit, but compose themselves, embrace the challenge, and allow the storm to make them better. How do you handle stress or setbacks?

Do you become a victim or a victor? Yes, the challenges happen to us, but we don't have to be a victim to our circumstances.

One of the most powerful things that I learned at work was the practice of Undisturbed Composure. When I get out

187

of bed before my feet hit the ground, I declare that I walk in undisturbed composure. Notice, I must release those words out into the atmosphere because I know that disturbances will come into my life, my job, and my home at times, but I have a choice to be a victor or a victim. I choose to shift my atmosphere and not let my atmosphere shift me. Your workplace can be an escort to your greatness, so don't despise your occupation. Allow your occupation to merge with your vocation and your gift will make room for you and bring you before great people!

Contact Information:
Pastor Charlene Johnson
(916) 502-2518
Email: reallifetransformationcenter@gmail.com
www.reallifetransformationcenter.com

CHAPTER SEVENTEEN

**Success Builders:
When the *BOSS needs help***

Diana Martinez, Author

According to the Merriam-Webster dictionary's official website, a 'boss' is defined as "a person who exercises control or authority; specifically: one who directs or supervises workers" ("Boss", 2019). The word "boss" has even colloquially been used as a way to describe a person who demonstrates an air of confidence or self-assurance and is able to succeed at most anything, they set their mind to. What the word itself ultimately boils down to is this: a boss is a person who can successfully lead a person or group of people in a task or through an event with a confidence in themselves as well as those they have been selected to lead.

A boss can be a supervisor or manager, a C.E.O., the leader of a military unit or simply even the director of movie. A boss is typically a person whose position gives them a certain measure of authority over others, whether they be in charge of a group of people who are required to follow the instructions of a designated boss or a group of people who have volunteered to follow those instructions. Because of this, a boss is expected to successfully lead their designated group with appropriate authority and to communicate in a clear and concise manner any instructions they may need to deliver to their group, regardless of how large or small that group may be. However, not all bosses are equipped with an inherent ability to effectively lead. Even bosses need help every now and again, but there is not always a resource available to them to obtain that help. That's where I come in.

I coach business owners, leaders, managers or anyone who desires to improve their communication skills between themselves and their teams in order to be successful and profitable. I myself have been a successful manager and leader in the work place, at church, and even in little league baseball for several years. I enjoy coaching others on how to succeed in the position they are in or are seeking. Through my own experiences, I have cultivated and perfected several strategies and skill sets that have given me much success in my various leadership roles throughout the years. I will now share a small handful of those experiences and the lessons I learned through them.

I have worked for the State of California for over 18 years, and for some of those years I worked in a managerial or supervisory role. Throughout my life, I have often been the designated boss for groups or for events, and I have even been "team mom" for some of my children's teams. Because of these leadership opportunities, I have learned much along the way. Two things I have learned that seem to be universal regardless of who or what I'm leading is this: 1) No matter how you lead or who you lead, a boss is expected to know the answer to *everything*, and 2) you must treat everyone with respect and keep your cool when things get hot.

Each time I was selected to be a lead or boss, I learned something new about communicating with people. People tend to be varied. There are so many types of personalities in the world, and navigating those personalities is sometimes a little difficult. Some people tend to be very easy to talk to and will follow the natural flow of the work or project they've been tasked with without issue. However, some people's personalities tend to be a little more difficult to work with. Learning to work with difficult personalities is not an easy task. There were times that I wanted to give up, to wash my hands of the situation and the people I was working with, but I knew that if the Lord opened the door for me to be in this position, He must have known that I could do it. I just needed to trust Him and seek Him in it. By having faith in Him and his plan for me, I was able to develop the art of learning people and how to effectively use their individual abilities to bring success to the team as a whole. I learned how to be patient, and the importance of listening to others and their ideas (even the crazy ideas). There were several times that I bit my tongue instead of dismissing someone and/or their proposals and was later grateful for choosing to do so. Sometimes I was simply not seeing the bigger picture.

While I learned much about others through my experiences and how to work effectively with those I met, I learned much more about myself than I ever did anyone else and was able to develop some skills that became useful in my role as a boss.

While learning how to successfully deal with the many different types of people I met, I also had to learn how to actually get the job done. Balancing people with workloads can become overwhelming at times. Setting goals and keeping a clear vision takes a strong sense of perseverance and, sometimes, letting go of people or things that are not working out. In this, I was able to learn how to better choose people for my teams. I became skilled at hiring or choosing people more effectively by way of interviewing or just through conversation, depending on the type of work or volunteer project. Even so, sometimes the people I chose didn't always work out, but I had a better grasp at choosing the best person for the task at hand.

When it came to larger projects, I sometimes needed help to manage the work as well as the people, so learning to pick out the right leaders to work under me and how to develop them was also a skill I needed to learn. The structure I developed throughout the years is a culmination of formal training, learning from others, seeking out more managerial skills on my own, and through the always popular method of "trial and error". To put it simply, I never gave up, even when I failed. I just tried something different until I succeeded!

Seeking guidance from Jesus was also very important to my success. It was amazing when He would reveal things to me in such a way that I knew it was Him pushing me and guiding me through those doors of opportunity.

It wasn't long before I noticed that not everyone managing the same type of teams I was managing were as successful I was. There were several occasions that people would say to me 'I wish I was on your team', or 'let me know when you are hiring because I want to work for you', or 'please include me in your next project'. While I took no joy in their current team's inability to function as a unit, I admit that it felt great to have those things said to me. It was validating to know that I was seen by those inside and outside of my team as an effective leader. I was certainly not the only successful manager or team leader, but there were just some who could not get their team together at all. It made me wonder what those leaders were doing differently than I was. In my observation, I noticed many differences. The two things that really stood out to me were the unsuccessful team leaders' communication and team building skills. These skills come easy to some but are much, much harder to grasp for others.

Some time ago, I was working with a team that was behind in production, had employees who had their pay being docked due to excessive absences without having enough leave credits to cover their time off, and had several issues with the employees' union. At first, I wondered what exactly I had gotten myself into. The difficulties I was facing sometimes seemed to be too much to overcome. The first thing I did was to pray for my team and ask that the Lord to guide me in handling them and all the issues I was facing at the time. Then, I decided to get better acquainted with my team by sitting with my team members learning a bit about what they did and how they processed their work from beginning to end. These impromptu meetings soon became official team meetings that often-included team building exercises. Through these meetings, I was able to set goals and schedule additional meetings, trainings, more team building exercises, and even used some of the ideas given to me by my team members. Soon after, I started to see the back log of work go down; in a matter of just a few months, the back log was completely gone! People started coming to work regularly, on time, and were no longer having their pay docked because of their excessive absenteeism. They started working as a team with me which in turn caused many of the union issues to disappear. It was amazing how fast the atmosphere started to change.

I was so proud of my team, and they knew it because I didn't hesitate to show my pride to them. I was also proud of myself for not giving up and for relying on Jesus to help me through the process. I knew that I could not have gotten through everything alone and needed guidance from Him. Praise the Lord!

No matter the type of business you run or the team you lead, the success of each enterprise ultimately relies on that enterprise's leader and his or her ability to adequately lead and direct their team to success. Without a capable leader, their business or team can crumble. In order for a boss to be successful, they must have great communication and team building skills.

Always remember that there are two bosses in every business or event: the boss you think you are, and the boss your team sees you as. Perception is a large part of being a successful boss. You must look, talk and walk like a boss; you must always carry yourself with confidence and authority, but also be able to talk to your team and communicate instructions and criticisms in an effective manner.

So, if you are a business owner, a manager, or someone building a team, then you are a boss! You may be the leader of a group for your church, a sales team or for your children's school or sports team; it doesn't matter what type of business you have or what type of team you lead, you are a B.O.S.S.: **B**ringing **O**ut **S**uccessful **S**trategies for your business or team.

The lessons I have learned throughout my experiences and shared here have been very successful for me. Seeking guidance from Jesus was also very important to my success. It was amazing when He would reveal things to me in such a way that I knew it was Him pushing me and guiding me through those doors of opportunity. I started my coaching business to teach these skills in depth to others to help them grow their business or position.

If you are interested in developing your skills to be that successful BOSS, here is my contact information:
Diana Martinez Business Owner, Author and Speaker.

Business information:
Success Builders
(916) 206-8128
Successbuilderstoday.com

Book information:

Comfortable in My Storm

By Diana Martinez

This book may be purchased directly from me, through Fabulousdiana.com or online through Amazon.com.

CHAPTER EIGHTEEN

Path of a Leader

Colette Nwonye, Author

Through some research, I discovered out-service training sessions. And if I were able to link the training to my professional growth, my employer would pay both tuition and travel costs. I took courses such as *Communication, Conflict Management, Developing Others, Interpersonal Skills, Team Development,* and others. I enjoyed learning practical leadership skills and meeting other supervisors and managers. However, when I took *Leading Effectively,* I learned that there is a difference between a manager and a leader. Managers use their position to command compliance from their staff and drive results. Whereas, leaders gain commitment from their followers by building relationships. As such, leaders are able to use their influence to reach organizational objectives. Budgetary restrictions eventually resulted in the elimination of all "non-mission critical" out-service training and travel. Though I was disappointed, I was motivated to search for alternative methods for continuing my leadership education and development as it was my heart's desire to become an effective leader.

Then one day, God answered my prayer. It was 2005. I was running to pick the girls up when I heard a commercial on a Christian radio channel. The melodic voice of a female, caught my attention as she described the university's accredited

Leadership and Organizational Studies graduate program. She also explained how the university facilitates courses from a faith-based perspective and offers them in the evening. I couldn't believe it! Within a few weeks, I attended an informational meeting. However, as a divorced working mother with two young children, I decided to delay my enrollment for several years. The girls were ten and seven years old when I finally applied and was accepted into the program.

Sometimes, I took the girls with me to the library. They would each sit at a workstation and do their homework using the computer, while I conducted research and worked on my master thesis. I still remember how, during one of our library trips, my youngest looked up at me and asked, "Mommy, when do we graduate?" I still laugh at her question. I finally graduated in 2010, earning a master's in Leadership and Organizational Studies.

In 2009, while still attending graduate school, God pushed me to a middle management position. I say pushed because I did not want to promote. I planned to finish school and get another job once I graduated. So, I resisted applying for the job until the final deadline; I called myself outsmarting God, so I reasoned that I was technically obedient when I applied for the position. However, when my employer offered a new promotional examination for the same classification. This was done to create a new certification list. I did not apply to take the examination.

To earn a spot on a certification list, individuals must take and successfully pass a promotional examination. Hiring managers use the certification list to select qualified individuals to interview for specific positions, and only those who score within the top three ranks are eligible to be interviewed. Now I was on the old certification list. My thought was that the hiring manager would select interviewees from the new certification list. Of course, God knew differently. So, imagine my surprise when I received a call to schedule an interview. I went so far as to tell the hiring manager that I did not take the new promotional examination. Therefore, I was not on the most recent certification list. She responded that since the job announcement for the position was posted when the new promotional examination was offered, the existing certification list would be used to select the interviewees. God let me know that He was still in charge and reminded me of His Word in Jeremiah 29:11 *"For I know the plans I have you," declares the LORD, "plans to prosper you and not to harm you, plans to give you hope and a future."*

Normally I prepare for interviews by researching the agency or company, familiarizing myself with the duty statement and creating a portfolio. The portfolio includes my most recent resume, my academic accomplishments, along with my accolades (e.g., certificates of Achievement or Appreciation, KUDOs, and letters of recommendations). However, I decided not to do of this this time, as I had purposed in my heart that I did not want to work for this manager.

Let me explain. In 2004, when I got promoted to management, I was working in the office with and for this particular manager. In all, six of us promoted to management at the same time. We were hired to open a new office and administer a history-making program. This program was the first of its kind in the nation. However, instead of my manager being proud that her office produced the majority of the managers to make this monumental event such a success, she let us know that by leaving we were not showing loyalty to her. She also let us know that we would not be welcome back in "her office."

I still remember that the evening before my scheduled interview. My mother was at my house, and I was crying. Yes, crying. I told her that "they didn't want me." Mama tried calmed me down and encouraging me to follow through with the interview. She reminded me that I tend to do well in interview settings. Still crying, I reluctantly agreed to attend my interview.

The following day, I once again contemplated withdrawing from the interview process. A few minutes before my interview, while sitting in my brown Dodge Caravan, I told God that I did not want to work for this manager. I explained that it didn't make sense for me to even go to the interview because the manager was not going to hire me anyway. As I continued to feel sorry for myself, I felt something heavy weigh down in my stomach. And Psalm 75:6-7 (KJV), came to mind *"For promotion cometh neither from the east, nor the west, nor from the south. But God is the judge: he putteth down one, and setteth up another."* Right after this, I felt something hot in my soul that said, "Who are you to turn down a promotion that I have set up for you." I immediately stopped crying. I knew without a doubt that this was God, Himself. Like for real. The feeling didn't make me afraid, but I felt a profound air of admonishment. However, defiant, I told God, that He would have to show me that it was His will for me to have this particular job. Also, I told Him that He would have to answer the interview questions. Yes, I was that ridiculously bold! And to this very day, I am not sure why the God of the Universe even put up with me.

As I walked into the office for my interview, I passed by my prior supervisor. A truly Christian woman, she was also interviewing for the position. She was walking out of the room as I was walking in. All of a sudden, she grabbed me. And while she hugged me, she whispered a prayer in my ear and said: "you better get this job." Once in the interview, I looked at each of the four panelists; one was the Deputy Director of our branch; another was the Division Chief. He reminded me of a grown-up Opie from *The Andy Griffith Show.* Then there was the Administrator for the region. The fourth panelist was the hiring manager. I looked every one of them in the eye, shook their hand, and said the obligatory, "thank you for this opportunity." If I'm honest, I truly do not remember what happened during the interview. And I was not surprised when I received a telephone call offering me the job. Now God had already dealt with me. So, I was on board and accepted the offer. However, I had to remind myself of God's Word to *"Be strong and courageous. Do not be afraid or terrified because of them, for the Lord your God goes with you; he will never leave you nor forsake you"* Deuteronomy 31:6 NIV.

So, on my first day of work, the office manager, and my new boss, straight out told me that I was not her first choice. That in fact, my prior manager, the one who hugged and prayed for me was. She went on to let me know that the other second-level manager, my new peer, was not thrilled that I was there either. My new manager made sure that I understood that although my counterpart and I were at the same level, my counterpart was "her Assistant Office Manager." She went on to explain that I would be to assist the clerical support staff. Second-level managers supervise first-level managers and first-level managers usually supervise clerical support staff. At any rate, I got my mind prepared to supervise the clerical support staff when my new boss further clarified that she wanted me to perform clerical support staff duties.

I complied and spent the first three weeks as a middle manager performing clerical support staff duties (e.g., filing correspondence, sorting and distributing mail, running copies, and answering telephones). I reminded myself, "*...that all things work together for them that love the God, to them who are called according to his purpose*" Romans 8:28 (NJV). So, performing these tasks didn't nearly bother me as much as it bothered the rank and file staff. They could not believe that as an upper-level manager, I was filing. More than a few of the staff asked, "Why are you filing?" then "Are they serious?" I tried to remain neutral by making a joke out of it, but I think my expression conveyed a lot. Disgusted, they would walk away shaking their heads from side-to-side.

I continued to perform clerical duties, until one day the Administrator for the region, my manager's boss, noticed me filing correspondence. She asked me why I was filing and how long I had been doing it. I answered. Then she asked me whether any of the first-level managers had been assigned to report to me. I told her the truth and answered none of them. She responded, "I am not paying you a manager's salary to do clerical work" and then walked off. The following day, my manager assigned three managers to me. My manager later explained that she wanted to make sure that "her mangers were humble" and still remembered how to do "the work." I had to laugh, here I didn't want the promotion, and she didn't want to promote me. So, one could say that she demoted me to clerical. What does Hebrews 12:6 NKJV say? *"For whom the Lord loves He chastens, And scourges every son whom He receives."* All I can say, is that God has a way making you understand that He means business. Won't He do it? Yes, He will and did.

So, once I was assigned my managers, I used the knowledge that I secured during graduate school to coach them. For example, I held bi-monthly one-on-one meetings with them. During these meetings, we would identify how they could align their behaviors with the strategic goals of the department and branch; we discussed their short-term and long-term career objectives and other topics. My goal was to create a learning organization where everyone in my section learned from one another, received coaching, and was mentored and grew together.

Eventually, I convinced my manager to allow the office to have regularly scheduled monthly all-staff meetings. I explained that this would provide an opportunity to share information with staff. I also pushed for us to have regularly scheduled monthly unit meetings. I suggested that we provide refresher training as well as offer developmental activities during these meetings. Further, I suggested that we use these meetings as an opportunity to develop staff by allowing them to facilitate the meetings, to take and disseminate the meeting notes, as well ensure that the meetings began and ended on time. Staff were engaged and took ownership of the meetings. They repeatedly expressed their appreciation of having both the all-staff and unit meetings where they could get information and learn new skills. They told me that they "knew that I was the reason and thanked me."

Consequently, sometime after the promotion, I was speaking with the Administrator about my interview. She explained that I did so well, that if I had the worst reference check ever, I would still outscore the other candidates. It was then that I realized that the promotion that I had so adamantly ran from was not about me at all. It was about my Father's work. My managerial position was and still is, a ministry. And as ministries go, when God had something else in mind, they tend to grow.

So, in 2011, after receiving numerous requests, I ran for President of the local chapter of an international professional workforce organization, and I won. The organization provides its members with personal and professional development opportunities through educational conferences, workshops, and other activities. Many of our employees and managers are members of the organization. I decided to use this platform to provide membership with opportunities to develop their leadership skills and prepare for promotion by creating a Lunch and Learn Program. The program has been well received and attended. And eight years later, it continues to offer lunch and learn sessions. A few months ago, I received an email from one of the organization's members that read, "*Good morning, I just wanted to share my good news with you! I could not have made the leap without your consistent encouragement and your willingness to share your vast professional and personal knowledge and experience with me. I look forward to the next time I see you in person so I can give you a big thank you hug!*"

Christian CEOs, I did not set out to lead anyone. However, I have since come to learn that leadership is a calling. When one answers the call to leadership, you never know who will be blessed. So, whether you are an intrapreneur while working for a company or an entrepreneur and working for yourself, remember to partner with God. Ask Him to coach and lead you down the road less traveled it will take to your path to leadership.

In September 1994, I began working for one of the largest public administrative agencies in the nation as less than a full-time employee. Then in 2004, I was promoted to management. I was placed on a 12-month probationary period and attended the 80-hour mandatory Basic Supervision Training (BST). After BST, I received no follow-up or refresher supervisorial or managerial-related training. Moreover, apart from quarterly probationary discussions, I received minimal to no one-on-one coaching or mentoring. So, I began a quest to learn how to coach and mentor myself.

Through some research, I discovered out-service training sessions. And if I were able to link the training to my professional growth, my employer would pay both tuition and travel costs. I took courses such as *Communication, Conflict Management, Developing Others, Interpersonal Skills, Team Development,* and others. I enjoyed learning practical leadership skills and meeting other supervisors and managers. However, when I took *Leading Effectively,* I learned that there is a difference between a manager and a leader. Managers use their position to command compliance from their staff and drive results. Whereas, leaders gain commitment from their followers by building relationships. As such, leaders are able to use their influence to reach organizational objectives. Budgetary restrictions eventually resulted in the elimination of all "non-mission critical" out-service training and travel. Though I was disappointed, I was motivated to search for alternative methods for continuing my leadership education and development as it was my heart's desire to become an effective leader.

Then one day, God answered my prayer. It was 2005. I was running to pick the girls up when I heard a commercial on a Christian radio channel. The melodic voice of a female, caught my attention as she described the university's accredited Leadership and Organizational Studies graduate program. She also explained how the university facilitates courses from a faith-based perspective and offers them in the evening. I couldn't believe it! Within a few weeks, I attended an informational meeting. However, as a divorced working mother with two young children, I decided to delay my enrollment for several years. The girls were ten and seven years old when I finally applied and was accepted into the program.

Sometimes, I took the girls with me to the library. They would each sit at a workstation and do their homework using the computer, while I conducted research and worked on my master thesis. I still remember how, during one of our library trips, my youngest looked up at me and asked, "Mommy, when do we graduate?" I still laugh at her question. I finally graduated in 2010, earning a master's in Leadership and Organizational Studies.

In 2009, while still attending graduate school, God pushed me to a middle management position. I say pushed because I did not want to promote. I planned to finish school and get another job once I graduated. So, I resisted applying for the job until the final deadline; I called myself outsmarting God, so I reasoned that I was technically obedient when I applied for the position. However, when my employer offered a new promotional examination for the same classification. This was done to create a new certification list. I did not apply to take the examination.

To earn a spot on a certification list, individuals must take and successfully pass a promotional examination. Hiring managers use the certification list to select qualified individuals to interview for specific positions, and only those who score within the top three ranks are eligible to be interviewed. Now I was on the old certification list. My thought was that the hiring manager would select interviewees from the new certification list. Of course, God knew differently. So, imagine my surprise when I received a call to schedule an interview. I went so far as to tell the hiring manager that I did not take the new promotional examination. Therefore, I was not on the most recent certification list. She responded that since the job announcement for the position was posted when the new promotional examination was offered, the existing certification list would be used to select the interviewees. God let me know that He was still in charge and reminded me of His Word in Jeremiah 29:11 *"For I know the plans I have you," declares the*

LORD, *"plans to prosper you and not to harm you, plans to give you hope and a future."*

Normally I prepare for interviews by researching the agency or company, familiarizing myself with the duty statement and creating a portfolio. The portfolio includes my most recent resume, my academic accomplishments, along with my accolades (e.g., certificates of Achievement or Appreciation, KUDOs, and letters of recommendations). However, I decided not to do of this this time, as I had purposed in my heart that I did not want to work for this manager.

Let me explain. In 2004, when I got promoted to management, I was working in the office with and for this particular manager. In all, six of us promoted to management at the same time. We were hired to open a new office and administer a history-making program. This program was the first of its kind in the nation. However, instead of my manager being proud that her office produced the majority of the managers to make this monumental event such a success, she let us know that by leaving we were not showing loyalty to her. She also let us know that we would not be welcome back in "her office."

I still remember that the evening before my scheduled interview. My mother was at my house, and I was crying. Yes, crying. I told her that "they didn't want me." Mama tried calmed me down and encouraging me to follow through with the interview. She reminded me that I tend to do well in interview settings. Still crying, I reluctantly agreed to attend my interview.

The following day, I once again contemplated withdrawing from the interview process. A few minutes before my interview, while sitting in my brown Dodge Caravan, I told God that I did not want to work for this manager. I explained that it didn't make sense for me to even go to the interview because the manager was not going to hire me anyway. As I continued to feel sorry for myself, I felt something heavy weigh down in my stomach. And Psalm 75:6-7 (KJV), came to mind *"For promotion cometh neither from the east, nor the west, nor from the south. But God is the judge: he putteth down one, and setteth up another."* Right after this, I felt something hot in my soul that said, "Who are you to turn down a promotion that I have set up for you." I immediately stopped crying. I knew without a doubt that this was God, Himself. Like for real. The feeling didn't make me afraid, but I felt a profound air of admonishment. However, defiant, I told God, that He would have to show me that it was His will for me to have this particular job. Also, I told Him that He would have to answer the interview questions. Yes, I was that ridiculously bold! And to this very day, I am not sure why the God of the Universe even put up with me.

As I walked into the office for my interview, I passed by my prior supervisor. A truly Christian woman, she was also interviewing for the position. She was walking out of the room as I was walking in. All of a sudden, she grabbed me. And while she hugged me, she whispered a prayer in my ear and said: "you better get this job." Once in the interview, I looked at each of the four panelists; one was the Deputy Director of our branch; another was the Division Chief. He reminded me of a grown-up Opie from *The Andy Griffith Show*. Then there was the Administrator for the region. The fourth panelist was the hiring manager. I looked every one of them in the eye, shook their hand, and said the obligatory, "thank you for this opportunity." If I'm honest, I truly do not remember what happened during the interview. And I was not surprised when I received a telephone call offering me the job. Now God had already dealt with me. So, I was on board and accepted the offer. However, I had to remind myself of God's Word to *"Be strong and courageous. Do not be afraid or terrified because of them, for the Lord your God goes with you; he will never leave you nor forsake you"* Deuteronomy 31:6 NIV.

So, on my first day of work, the office manager, and my new boss, straight out told me that I was not her first choice. That in fact, my prior manager, the one who hugged and prayed for me was. She went on to let me know that the other second-level manager, my new peer, was not thrilled that I was there either. My new manager made sure that I understood that although my counterpart and I were at the same level, my counterpart was "her Assistant Office Manager." She went on to explain that I would be to assist the clerical support staff. Second-level managers supervise first-level managers and first-level managers usually supervise clerical support staff. At any rate, I got my mind prepared to supervise the clerical support staff when my new boss further clarified that she wanted me to perform clerical support staff duties.

I complied and spent the first three weeks as a middle manager performing clerical support staff duties (e.g., filing correspondence, sorting and distributing mail, running copies, and answering telephones). I reminded myself, "*...that all things work together for them that love the God, to them who are called according to his purpose*" Romans 8:28 (NJV). So, performing these tasks didn't nearly bother me as much as it bothered the rank and file staff. They could not believe that as an upper-level manager, I was filing. More than a few of the staff asked, "Why are you filing?" then "Are they serious?" I tried to remain neutral by making a joke out of it, but I think my expression conveyed a lot. Disgusted, they would walk away shaking their heads from side-to-side.

I continued to perform clerical duties, until one day the Administrator for the region, my manager's boss, noticed me filing correspondence. She asked me why I was filing and how long I had been doing it. I answered. Then she asked me whether any of the first-level managers had been assigned to report to me. I told her the truth and answered none of them. She responded, "I am not paying you a manager's salary to do clerical work" and then walked off. The following day, my manager assigned three managers to me. My manager later explained that she wanted to make sure that "her mangers were humble" and still remembered how to do "the work." I had to laugh, here I didn't want the promotion, and she didn't want to promote me. So, one could say that she demoted me to clerical. What does Hebrews 12:6 NKJV say? *"For whom the Lord loves He chastens, And scourges every son whom He receives."* All I can say, is that God has a way making you understand that He means business. Won't He do it? Yes, He will and did.

So, once I was assigned my managers, I used the knowledge that I secured during graduate school to coach them. For example, I held bi-monthly one-on-one meetings with them. During these meetings, we would identify how they could align their behaviors with the strategic goals of the department and branch; we discussed their short-term and long-term career objectives and other topics. My goal was to create a learning organization where everyone in my section learned from one another, received coaching, and was mentored and grew together.

Eventually, I convinced my manager to allow the office to have regularly scheduled monthly all-staff meetings. I explained that this would provide an opportunity to share information with staff. I also pushed for us to have regularly scheduled monthly unit meetings. I suggested that we provide refresher training as well as offer developmental activities during these meetings. Further, I suggested that we use these meetings as an opportunity to develop staff by allowing them to facilitate the meetings, to take and disseminate the meeting notes, as well ensure that the meetings began and ended on time. Staff were engaged and took ownership of the meetings. They repeatedly expressed their appreciation of having both the all-staff and unit meetings where they could get information and learn new skills. They told me that they "knew that I was the reason and thanked me."

Consequently, sometime after the promotion, I was speaking with the Administrator about my interview. She explained that I did so well, that if I had the worst reference check ever, I would still outscore the other candidates. It was then that I realized that the promotion that I had so adamantly ran from was not about me at all. It was about my Father's work. My managerial position was and still is, a ministry. And as ministries go, when God had something else in mind, they tend to grow.

So, in 2011, after receiving numerous requests, I ran for President of the local chapter of an international professional workforce organization, and I won. The organization provides its members with personal and professional development opportunities through educational conferences, workshops, and other activities. Many of our employees and managers are members of the organization. I decided to use this platform to provide membership with opportunities to develop their leadership skills and prepare for promotion by creating a Lunch and Learn Program. The program has been well received and attended. And eight years later, it continues to offer lunch and learn sessions. A few months ago, I received an email from one of the organization's members that read, "*Good morning, I just wanted to share my good news with you! I could not have made the leap without your consistent encouragement and your willingness to share your vast professional and personal knowledge and experience with me. I look forward to the next time I see you in person so I can give you a big thank you hug!*"

Christian CEOs, I did not set out to lead anyone. However, I have since come to learn that leadership is a calling. When one answers the call to leadership, you never know who will be blessed. So, whether you are an intrapreneur while working for a company or an entrepreneur and working for yourself, remember to partner with God. Ask Him to coach and lead you down the road less traveled it will take to your path to leadership.

Contact Information:
Colette Nwoyne
(559) 970-9494
Email: Colette.nwonye@gmail.com
Instagram: @ColetteNwonye

ABOUT THE VISIONARY

Sheya Atterbery-Chisenga

Sheya Atterberry-Chisenga is a Small Business Owner, Empowerment Coach, Author and Visionary of several book compilations. Sheya is known in the coaching industry for using her faith to activate God's blessings in her life. She started her own coaching business, It's My Time to Rise Business Institute and Entrepreneurial Center for Women, where she conducts live workshops, mastermind sessions and yearly conferences to inspire women to "Answer the Call" that supports the freedom and lifestyle they desire. Whether you have been in business, ministry or your career for several years or, you are soul searching, the advice, resources and tools Sheya has developed will help you build a rewarding and enjoyable life.

She has been an entrepreneur and has worked in church ministry for over 22 years. When she first started her coaching business in January of 2009, she didn't have a clue about she was supposed to do. Through her struggles, she became clear on who she was called to serve and how to earn a consistent income. Sheya serves faithfully in her church and community and shares a home with her husband of 10 years, and their beautiful daughter, Rose Chisenga.

If you are interested in Sheya Atterberry-Chisenga conducting a seminar, a workshop or, to schedule a speaking engagement, please call (916) 209 - 0367 or go to her website at www.sheyachisenga.com.

Made in the
USA
Lexington, KY